Spaghetti and Meatballs, page 44

Cooking Light®

Pasta

Oxmoor House®

ISBN: 0-8487-3065-8
Library of Congress Control Number:
2006921190
Printed in the United States of America
First printing 2006

Be sure to check with your health-care provider
before making any changes in your diet.

Oxmoor House, Inc.
Editor in Chief: Nancy Fitzpatrick Wyatt
Executive Editor: Katherine M. Eakin
Copy Chief: Allison Long Lowery

Cooking Light Pasta
Editor: Terri Laschober
Food Editors: Anne Cain, M.S., R.D.;
    Alyson Moreland Haynes
Copy Editor: Jacqueline Giovanelli
Editorial Assistants: Julie Boston;
    Brigette Gaucher
Photography Director: Jim Bathie
Senior Photo Stylist: Kay E. Clarke
Photo Stylist: Katherine Eckert
Director, Test Kitchens: Elizabeth Tyler Austin
Assistant Director, Test Kitchens:
    Julie Christopher
Test Kitchens Staff: Kristi Carter,
    Nicole Lee Faber, Kathleen Royal Phillips,
    Elise Weis, Kelley Self Wilton
Director of Production: Laura Lockhart
Publishing Systems Administrator: Rick Tucker
Production Manager: Greg A. Amason
Production Assistant: Faye Porter Bonner

Contributors:
Designer: Carol Damsky
Indexer: Mary Ann Laurens
Editorial Interns: Rachel Quinlivan, R.D.;
    Mary Catherine Shamblin;
    Vanessa Rusch Thomas; Ashley Wells
Photographers: Beau Gustafson, Lee Harrelson
Photo Stylist: Lydia DeGaris-Pursell

To order additional publications, call
1-800-765-6400, or visit **oxmoorhouse.com**

CONTENTS

Essential Pasta   8

These dishes come to mind when we
hear the word "pasta." From a basic
fettuccine Alfredo to an elegant
carbonara, here are our best recipes for
the classics that no *Cooking Light* cook
should be without.

Family Favorites   30

Down-home mac and cheese,
comforting casseroles, and warming
soups—we offer recipes to nourish your
family and your soul.

Dinner Tonight   50

Looking for quick-and-easy dinner
solutions? Toss pasta with any of these
simple combinations of ingredients and
presto! Dinner is served.

Casual Entertaining 72

With fancy presentations to entice the eye and complex flavors to delight the palate, these recipes are sure to impress. We think you'll find that pasta is the perfect blank canvas to show off your culinary talents to your guests.

Salads 94

From Asian noodle salads to fresh combinations bursting with summer flavor, pasta is quite at home in a salad. Served warm or cold, these recipes will hit the spot for a light lunch or supper.

World Cuisine 114

Whether a time-honored dish or a new fusion of ethnic ingredients, pasta brings together the best from around the globe. You'll find everything from healthier versions of your favorite Chinese take-out dishes to an exotic dish from the continent of Africa.

Cooking Light

Editor in Chief: Mary Kay Culpepper
Executive Editor: Billy R. Sims
Art Director: Susan Waldrip Dendy
Managing Editor: Maelynn Cheung
Senior Food Editor: Alison Mann Ashton
Senior Editor: Anamary Pelayo
Features Editor: Phillip Rhodes
Projects Editor: Mary Simpson Creel, M.S., R.D.
Associate Food Editors: Timothy Q. Cebula,
    Ann Taylor Pittman
Assistant Food Editor: Kathy C. Kitchens, R.D.
Assistant Editor: Cindy Hatcher
Contributing Beauty Editor: Carol Straley
Test Kitchens Director: Vanessa Taylor Johnson
Food Stylist: Kellie Gerber Kelley
Assistant Food Stylist: M. Kathleen Kanen
Test Kitchens Professionals: Sam Brannock,
    Kathryn Conrad, Mary H. Drennen,
    Jan Jacks Moon, Tiffany Vickers,
    Mike Wilson
Assistant Art Director: Maya Metz Logue
Senior Designers: Fernande Bondarenko,
    J. Shay McNamee
Designer: Brigette Mayer
Senior Photographers: Becky Luigart-Stayner,
    Randy Mayor
Senior Photo Stylist: Cindy Barr
Photo Stylists: Melanie J. Clarke, Jan Gautro
Digital Photo Stylist: Jan A. Smith
Studio Assistant: Celine Chenoweth
Copy Chief: Maria Parker Hopkins
Senior Copy Editor: Susan Roberts
Copy Editor: Johannah Paiva
Production Manager: Liz Rhoades
Production Editors: Joanne McCrary Brasseal,
    Hazel R. Eddins
Administrative Coordinator: Carol D. Johnson
Office Manager: Rita K. Jackson
Editorial Assistants: Melissa Hoover,
    Brandy Rushing
Correspondence Editor: Michelle Gibson Daniels
Interns: Rachel Cardina, Marie Hegler,
    Emily Self

CookingLight.com
Editor: Jennifer Middleton Richards
Online Producer: Abigail Masters

Cover: *Pappardelle with Tomatoes, Arugula, and Parmesan* (page 108)

Welcome

Pasta is adaptable, dependable, and just plain enjoyable. But there's another thing that pasta is, and that's essential. For a *Cooking Light*® cook, pasta is perhaps the one staple we always have in our pantries.

In this cookbook, you'll find the pasta recipes we believe to be the essential recipes for every *Cooking Light* cook. These recipes are our tried-and-true classics—ones we love to make again and again.

Each chapter offers mouthwatering, flavorful recipes, complete with nutritional analyses that will help you to cook delicious dishes that, of course, are better for you. After all, we think that eating smart, being fit, and living well are the essentials to the *Cooking Light* way of life.

So whether you're looking for a recipe for comforting Turkey Tetrazzini, or something a little more dazzling, such as Scallops and Pasta with Pistachio-Parsley Pesto, you're sure to find it in this edition of *The Cooking Light Cook's Essential Recipe Collection*. I hope these recipes will become essentials to your family, just as they are to the staff at *Cooking Light*.

Very truly yours,

Mary Kay Culpepper
Editor in Chief

essential
pasta

Fettuccine Alfredo

1 pound uncooked fettuccine
1 tablespoon butter
1¼ cups half-and-half
¾ cup (3 ounces) grated fresh
   Parmesan cheese
½ teaspoon salt
¼ teaspoon black pepper

1. Cook pasta according to package directions, omitting salt and fat.
2. Melt butter in a large skillet over medium heat. Add half-and-half, cheese, salt, and pepper; cook 1 minute, stirring constantly. Reduce heat; add pasta, tossing gently to coat. Yield: 6 servings (serving size: 1½ cups).

CALORIES 427 (31% from fat); FAT 14.6g (sat 7.8g, mono 4.2g, poly 1.3g); PROTEIN 17.2g; CARB 56.5g; FIBER 2.1g; CHOL 105mg; IRON 3.6mg; SODIUM 479mg; CALC 245mg

Fettuccine, which translates to "small ribbons," is the perfect match for Alfredo because the smooth sauce can easily coat the long strands. Use a spoon to help swirl the noodles neatly onto your fork.

Fettuccine Alfredo was created in the 1920s by Roman restaurateur Alfredo di Lello. In our version of this rich, creamy dish, we used half-and-half instead of whipping cream and decreased the amount of butter and cheese ever so slightly to lower the fat by about 10 grams per serving.

Spaghetti with Marinara Sauce

1 tablespoon olive oil
1½ tablespoons minced garlic
6 pounds coarsely chopped
    peeled tomato (about 6
    cups)
¾ teaspoon salt
½ teaspoon black pepper
¼ cup chopped fresh basil
¼ cup chopped fresh parsley
8 cups hot cooked spaghetti
    (about 1 pound uncooked
    pasta)

1. Heat oil in a large saucepan over medium heat. Add garlic; cook 2 minutes, stirring frequently. Add tomato, salt, and pepper; bring to a boil. Reduce heat; simmer 25 minutes, stirring occasionally. Stir in basil and parsley, and cook 1 minute. Serve over pasta. Yield: 6 servings (serving size: 1 cup sauce and 1⅓ cups pasta).

CALORIES 384 (12% from fat); FAT 5.1g (sat 0.7g, mono 2g, poly 1.3g); PROTEIN 13.1g; CARB 75.1g; FIBER 8.4g; CHOL 0mg; IRON 5mg; SODIUM 338mg; CALC 48mg

To peel tomatoes, use a small paring knife to score the bottom of each tomato with an "X," cutting just through the skin but not into the flesh. Place the tomatoes in a pot of boiling water for 30 seconds. Remove them with a slotted spoon; quickly plunge the tomatoes into a bowl of ice water to stop the cooking. Once they've cooled, you can easily peel away the skins from the tomatoes.

Although there are many explanations of what marinara is and how it's made, our version sticks to this definition: a very simple fresh tomato sauce with garlic and olive oil. The salt, pepper, and fresh herbs intensify and complement the flavor of the tomatoes.

Grilled Vegetable Lasagna

The best vegetables for grilling are sturdy ones such as eggplant, yellow squash, zucchini, tomatoes, bell peppers, onions, and potatoes. Depending on the recipe, you can grill the vegetables first, then slice them, or slice them before grilling. If the vegetables are large enough, place them directly on the grill. For smaller pieces, use a grill basket or skewers. No matter your method, grilling vegetables adds depth of flavor, sweetness, and appealing chargrilled appearance.

3 eggplants, cut lengthwise into ¼-inch slices (about 3 pounds)
3 zucchini, cut lengthwise into ⅛-inch slices (about 1¼ pounds)
Cooking spray
1 teaspoon salt, divided
¾ teaspoon freshly ground black pepper, divided
2 red bell peppers, quartered and seeded
1 (15-ounce) container fat-free ricotta cheese
1 large egg, lightly beaten
¾ cup (3 ounces) grated Asiago cheese, divided
¼ cup minced fresh basil
¼ cup minced fresh parsley
9 uncooked lasagna noodles, divided
1 (26-ounce) jar tomato-basil pasta sauce (such as Muir Glen)
¾ cup (3 ounces) shredded part-skim mozzarella cheese
¼ cup commercial pesto (such as Alessi)

1. Preheat grill.
2. Coat eggplant and zucchini slices with cooking spray. Sprinkle with ½ teaspoon salt and ¼ teaspoon black pepper. Grill eggplant and zucchini 1½ minutes on each side or just until tender. Cool; combine in a large bowl.
3. Place bell peppers on grill, skin-side down; grill 3 minutes or until tender. Cut into 1-inch-wide strips. Add bell peppers to eggplant mixture.
4. Combine ricotta cheese, egg, ½ cup Asiago cheese, basil, parsley, remaining ½ teaspoon salt, and remaining ½ teaspoon black pepper.
5. Cook lasagna noodles according to package directions, omitting salt and fat.
6. Preheat oven to 375°.
7. Spread ½ cup pasta sauce in a 13 x 9–inch baking dish coated with cooking spray. Arrange 3 noodles over sauce. Top with half of eggplant mixture. Spread half of ricotta cheese mixture over eggplant mixture; sprinkle with ¼ cup mozzarella cheese.
8. Arrange 3 noodles and 1 cup pasta sauce over cheese; cover with remaining eggplant mixture. Top with remaining ricotta mixture. Spread pesto over ricotta, and sprinkle with ¼ cup mozzarella cheese. Cover with 3 noodles.
9. Spoon 1 cup pasta sauce over noodles. Sprinkle with remaining ¼ cup Asiago cheese and ¼ cup mozzarella cheese.
10. Bake at 375° for 1 hour. Let stand 15 minutes before serving. Yield: 10 servings.

CALORIES 318 (29% from fat); FAT 10.4g (sat 4.2g, mono 1.3g, poly 0.4g); PROTEIN 15.2g; CARB 41.9g; FIBER 3.2g; CHOL 40mg; IRON 2.7mg; SODIUM 728mg; CALC 269mg

Grilled vegetables move from side dish to center stage in this vegetarian entrée. To speed preparation, use no-boil lasagna noodles; the baking time remains the same.

Pasta Primavera

Although not usually considered a staple in light cooking, whipping cream is key to achieving rich flavor in this recipe. Because it's used in a small amount as an enhancing ingredient rather than as a base, the cream adds flavor without adding too many calories. Also, the higher-fat content of whipping cream means there's less chance of curdling when heated.

8 ounces uncooked fusilli (short twisted spaghetti)
2 cups (1-inch) diagonally cut thin asparagus (about ¾ pound)
½ cup shelled green peas (about ¾ pound unshelled green peas)
1 teaspoon olive oil
Cooking spray
1 small yellow bell pepper, cut into julienne strips
1 small red onion, thinly sliced
2 garlic cloves, minced
1 cup halved cherry tomatoes
⅔ cup fat-free, less-sodium chicken broth
⅓ cup whipping cream
½ teaspoon salt
½ teaspoon crushed red pepper
¼ cup (1 ounce) shredded fresh Parmesan cheese
¼ cup thinly sliced fresh basil

1. Cook pasta according to package directions, omitting salt and fat. Add asparagus and peas during last minute of cooking. Drain; place in a large bowl.
2. Heat oil in a large nonstick skillet coated with cooking spray over medium-high heat. Add bell pepper, onion, and garlic; sauté 5 minutes. Add tomatoes; sauté 1 minute. Stir in broth, whipping cream, salt, and red pepper; cook 2 minutes or until thoroughly heated.
3. Add tomato mixture to pasta mixture; toss to coat. Sprinkle with cheese and basil. Serve immediately. Yield: 4 servings (serving size: 1½ cups).

CALORIES 364 (28% from fat); FAT 11.2g (sat 6g, mono 3.4g, poly 0.6g); PROTEIN 14.1g; CARB 54g; FIBER 5.4g; CHOL 31mg; IRON 3.2mg; SODIUM 476mg; CALC 125mg

Tender asparagus and tiny fresh green peas are the quintessential ingredients in this Italian classic. When buying fresh peas, look for young, well-filled pods with a soft, velvety texture. Store unshelled peas uncovered in the refrigerator, and use them as soon as possible for the best flavor.

Shrimp Pad Thai

Fish sauce, widely used in southeast Asian cuisine as a condiment and flavoring for various dishes, is a salty, light-brown liquid made from fermented fish, water, and salt. It's best used sparingly—just a spoonful makes a world of difference in many dishes. Combine fish sauce with sugar and lime juice to make a dipping sauce for vegetables and spring rolls, or use it as a base to add pungent flavor, as in this dish.

½ pound wide rice stick
   noodles (banh pho)
¼ cup ketchup
3 tablespoons fish sauce
2 tablespoons sugar
½ teaspoon crushed red pepper
2 tablespoons vegetable oil,
   divided
1 pound medium shrimp,
   peeled and deveined
2 large eggs, lightly beaten
1 cup fresh bean sprouts
¾ cup (1-inch) sliced green
   onions
1 teaspoon bottled minced
   garlic
2 tablespoons chopped
   unsalted, dry-roasted
   peanuts

1. Place noodles in a large bowl. Add hot water to cover; let stand 12 minutes or until tender. Drain.
2. Combine ketchup, fish sauce, sugar, and pepper in a small bowl.
3. Heat 2 teaspoons oil in a large nonstick skillet over medium-high heat. Add shrimp; sauté 2 minutes or until shrimp are done. Remove shrimp from pan; keep warm.
4. Heat 4 teaspoons oil in pan over medium-high heat. Add eggs; cook 30 seconds or until soft-scrambled, stirring constantly. Add sprouts, green onions, and garlic; cook 1 minute. Add noodles, ketchup mixture, and shrimp; cook 3 minutes or until heated. Sprinkle with peanuts. Yield: 6 servings (serving size: 1½ cups).

CALORIES 343 (24% from fat); FAT 9.2g (sat 1.6g, mono 2.6g, poly 3.9g); PROTEIN 21.3g; CARB 42.4g; FIBER 1.4g; CHOL 186mg; IRON 3mg; SODIUM 912mg; CALC 60mg

Pad Thai is the most popular noodle dish in Thailand. This supereasy recipe is a variation of Thai restaurant fare. Substitute 4 cups hot cooked linguine for the rice stick noodles if you have trouble finding them.

Linguine with Clam Sauce

12 ounces uncooked linguine
3 tablespoons butter
5 garlic cloves, minced
½ cup dry white wine
½ teaspoon salt
1 (8-ounce) bottle clam juice
2 (6½-ounce) cans minced
   clams, undrained
24 littleneck clams, scrubbed
1 cup finely chopped parsley
2 tablespoons fresh lemon
   juice
⅛ teaspoon freshly ground
   black pepper
Lemon wedges

1. Cook linguine according to package directions, omitting salt and fat. Set aside.
2. Melt butter in a large skillet over medium heat. Add garlic to pan; cook 3 minutes or until golden.
3. Stir in wine, salt, and clam juice. Drain minced clams; add juice to pan (reserve minced clams). Simmer 5 minutes. Add littleneck clams; cover and cook 3 to 4 minutes or until shells open. Remove from heat, and discard any unopened shells. Add reserved minced clams, parsley, lemon juice, and pepper.
4. Place pasta in a large bowl. Add clam mixture to pasta, and toss well. Serve with lemon wedges. Yield: 6 servings (serving size: about 1 cup pasta mixture).

CALORIES 332 (19% from fat); FAT 7g (sat 3.8g, mono 1.7g, poly 0.3g); PROTEIN 17.1g; CARB 47.5g; FIBER 2.2g; CHOL 39mg; IRON 8.5mg; SODIUM 627mg; CALC 54mg

There are two main types of clams: soft shells and hard shells, but most of the clams sold in markets are hard-shell. Littleneck clams are the smallest variety and have the most tender meat. Buy clams in the shell alive, and look for shells that are clamped tight. (If you can open the shell easily, the clam is already dead.) Store live clams in a bowl draped with wet cloths in the refrigerator and cook within 2 days. Never store clams in a sealed plastic bag or on ice because they will die. For chowders and other dishes that use only the meat of the clams, canned clams, available whole or minced, are a good choice.

Commonly served in Calabria, a coastal region of Italy rich with fresh seafood, this dish joins minced clams and tender littleneck clams with white wine and garlic. Tossed with hearty linguine and served with lemon wedges and grilled asparagus, it embodies how fresh, simple ingredients can combine in perfect union.

Beef Stroganoff

When purchasing beef, look for a cherry red color, or—if it's vacuum-packed—a dark, purplish red color. The visible fat should be very white. The steak will be easier to slice if you partially freeze it first. Slice it diagonally across the grain into thin, 2-inch-long strips.

1 (8-ounce) carton reduced-fat sour cream
3 tablespoons no salt–added tomato paste
1 teaspoon Worcestershire sauce
½ cup all-purpose flour
1 teaspoon salt
⅛ teaspoon freshly ground black pepper
2 pounds boneless sirloin steak, cut into (2-inch) strips
1 tablespoon butter
½ cup chopped onion
1 (14-ounce) can less-sodium beef broth
2 cups sliced mushrooms
Chopped fresh parsley (optional)
8 cups hot cooked medium egg noodles (about 7 cups uncooked pasta)

1. Combine first 3 ingredients in a bowl. Set aside.
2. Combine flour, salt, and pepper in a large zip-top plastic bag. Add beef; seal and shake to coat beef.
3. Melt butter in a large nonstick skillet over medium-high heat. Add onion; sauté 2 minutes or until tender. Add beef and flour mixture; sauté 3 minutes or until beef is browned. Gradually add broth, scraping pan to loosen browned bits. Add mushrooms; cover and cook 5 minutes or until mushrooms are tender. Reduce heat to low; gradually stir in sour cream mixture. Cook, uncovered, 1 minute or until heated (do not boil). Stir in parsley, if desired. Serve over egg noodles. Yield: 8 servings (serving size: ¾ cup beef mixture and 1 cup noodles).

CALORIES 473 (30% from fat); FAT 16g (sat 7g, mono 4.3g, poly 1.1g); PROTEIN 30.2g; CARB 50.6g; FIBER 2.6g; CHOL 129mg; IRON 5.7mg; SODIUM 417mg; CALC 81mg

This traditional Russian dish is quick to prepare; use frozen chopped onions and presliced mushrooms to make it even faster. To maintain a creamy consistency, be careful not to bring the sauce to a boil once you stir in the sour cream mixture.

Beef Carbonnade

Cooking with beer is a unique technique for adding low-fat flavor to recipes. Most of the alcohol evaporates when cooked, leaving only the great taste behind. Dark beers add a more pungent, rich flavor, whereas light beers provide just a hint of mild beer flavor that makes an ordinary recipe simply delicious. In this recipe, a light brew perfectly mellows the stronger accents of bacon and thyme.

2 bacon slices, finely diced
2½ pounds boneless chuck roast, cut into 1-inch cubes
½ teaspoon salt
½ teaspoon black pepper
1 garlic clove, minced
5 cups thinly sliced onion (about 4 medium)
3 tablespoons all-purpose flour
2 teaspoons white wine vinegar
½ teaspoon sugar
½ teaspoon dried thyme
1 (10½-ounce) can beef broth
1 (12-ounce) bottle light beer
1 bay leaf
6 cups hot cooked wide egg noodles (about 12 ounces uncooked pasta)

1. Preheat oven to 325°.

2. Cook bacon in a large Dutch oven over medium-high heat until crisp; remove bacon, reserving drippings in pan. Set bacon aside. Add beef, salt, and pepper to drippings in pan; cook 5 minutes, browning beef well on all sides. Add garlic; cook 30 seconds. Remove beef from pan with a slotted spoon; set aside.

3. Add onion to pan; cover and cook over medium heat 10 minutes, stirring occasionally. Stir in flour; cook 2 minutes. Add vinegar and next 5 ingredients; bring to a boil. Return bacon and beef to pan. Cover and bake at 325° for 2 hours or until beef is tender. Discard bay leaf. Serve over noodles. Yield: 6 servings (serving size: 1 cup beef mixture and 1 cup noodles).

CALORIES 540 (26% from fat); FAT 15.3g (sat 5.4g, mono 6.1g, poly 1.8g); PROTEIN 43.3g; CARB 52.1g; FIBER 5.5g; CHOL 147mg; IRON 7.1mg; SODIUM 636mg; CALC 60mg

A staff favorite, this easy recipe relies on the age-old technique of braising, in which less tender cuts of meat, along with aromatic vegetables, slowly cook in liquid. The fork-tender beef will melt in your mouth.

Ragù Alla Bolognese with Fettuccine

The wine you choose for cooking anything other than desserts should generally be dry. The high sugar content in sweet wines can change the balance of flavors. The best all-around choice when a recipe calls for dry white wine is a quality American Sauvignon Blanc. Wine contributes flavors to the final dish, so don't be tempted to use anything of a lesser caliber. Also, remember that wine should act as a flavor enhancer; if you add too much, you can easily overwhelm a dish. If tasters say they hardly know its there, you've used just the right amount.

1 tablespoon olive oil
1 cup finely chopped onion
1 cup finely chopped celery
½ cup finely chopped carrot
5 ounces ground veal
5 ounces ground pork
5 ounces ground round
1 cup dry white wine
½ teaspoon salt
½ teaspoon black pepper
¼ teaspoon ground nutmeg
1 bay leaf
1 (14-ounce) can fat-free, less-sodium chicken broth
1 (10¾-ounce) can tomato purée
1 cup whole milk
2 tablespoons minced fresh flat-leaf parsley
2 (9-ounce) packages fresh fettuccine
2 tablespoons grated fresh Parmesan cheese
Parsley sprigs (optional)

1. Heat oil in a large Dutch oven over medium heat. Add onion, celery, and carrot; cover. Cook 8 minutes, stirring occasionally. Remove onion mixture from pan.

2. Add veal, pork, and beef to pan; cook over medium heat until browned, stirring to crumble. Add wine, salt, pepper, nutmeg, and bay leaf; bring to a boil. Cook 5 minutes. Add onion mixture, broth, and tomato purée; bring to a simmer. Cook 1 hour, stirring occasionally.

3. Stir in milk and minced parsley; bring to a boil. Reduce heat, and simmer 40 minutes. Discard bay leaf.

4. Cook pasta according to package directions, omitting salt and fat. Add pasta to meat sauce, and toss to coat. Sprinkle evenly with cheese. Garnish with parsley sprigs, if desired. Yield: 8 servings (serving size: 1½ cups).

CALORIES 369 (29% from fat); FAT 11.8g (sat 4.2g, mono 4.8g, poly 1.4g); PROTEIN 21.4g; CARB 44g; FIBER 4.2g; CHOL 87mg; IRON 3.7mg; SODIUM 546mg; CALC 117mg

Dating back to Renaissance times, ragù (or ragoût in France) had its start as a highly seasoned meat stew served by chefs in noble courts. It was first tossed with pasta in the early 1800s by cooks in what is now Italy's Emilia-Romagna region. While there are countless renditions of ragù, this version is adapted from the renowned sauce from the Italian city of Bologna.

Asparagus and Chicken Carbonara

Nutritionally, egg substitutes are essentially the same as egg whites because they're made from egg whites, corn oil, water, flavorings, and preservatives. Egg substitutes are excellent to use in recipes that traditionally call for raw eggs, such as this carbonara. Substitutes are pasteurized and have a low risk of containing bacteria, which means they don't have to be heated to 160°F to be safe to eat. It's not recommended to use egg substitutes in place of whole eggs in baking because they don't perform the same functions that whole eggs do.

8 ounces uncooked spaghetti
2 cups (1-inch) slices asparagus (about ¾ pound)
½ cup egg substitute
½ cup evaporated fat-free milk
2 teaspoons olive oil
½ cup chopped onion
¼ cup dry vermouth
2 cups chopped skinless, boneless rotisserie chicken breast
½ cup (2 ounces) grated fresh Parmesan cheese
3 tablespoons finely chopped fresh flat-leaf parsley
¾ teaspoon salt
½ teaspoon freshly ground black pepper
4 bacon slices, cooked and crumbled

1. Cook pasta in boiling water 10 minutes or until al dente; add asparagus during final 2 minutes of cooking. Drain pasta mixture in a colander over a bowl, reserving ⅓ cup cooking liquid. Combine reserved cooking liquid, egg substitute, and milk, stirring with a whisk.
2. Heat a large nonstick skillet over medium-high heat. Add oil and onion to pan; sauté 2 minutes. Add vermouth; cook 1 minute. Stir in pasta mixture. Remove from heat; stir in milk mixture, chicken, and cheese. Place pan over medium heat, and cook 4 minutes or until slightly thick, stirring frequently. Remove from heat; stir in parsley, salt, pepper, and bacon. Serve immediately. Yield: 5 servings (serving size: about 1¼ cups).

CALORIES 416 (23% from fat); FAT 10.8g (sat 3.7g, mono 4.4g, poly 2g); PROTEIN 34.7g; CARB 41.9g; FIBER 3.1g; CHOL 60mg; IRON 3.4mg; SODIUM 700mg; CALC 236mg

Pasta carbonara is traditionally made with raw egg yolks and whipping cream. This lighter version achieves the same texture with egg substitute and fat-free evaporated milk. Serve this dish immediately; if it stands, the sauce can become too thick.

family favorites

Creamy Four-Cheese Macaroni

Melba toast, a very thinly sliced crisp toast, was named after Dame Nellie Melba, the stage name of Australian opera singer Helen Porter Mitchell. In 1897 when the singer was very ill, this toast became a staple in her diet. Often found on top of soups and salads or as an accompaniment to dips and spreads, the toasts pack flavor without adding many calories or much fat. The crispiness of the toasts is a wonderful contrast to the creamy cheese and tender noodles in this recipe.

⅓ cup all-purpose flour
2⅔ cups 1% low-fat milk
¾ cup (3 ounces) shredded fontina or Swiss cheese
½ cup (2 ounces) grated fresh Parmesan cheese
½ cup (2 ounces) shredded extrasharp Cheddar cheese
3 ounces light processed cheese, cubed (such as Velveeta Light)
6 cups cooked elbow macaroni (about 3 cups uncooked)
¼ teaspoon salt
Cooking spray
⅓ cup crushed onion Melba toasts (about 4 [3½-inch] toasts)
1 tablespoon butter, softened

1. Preheat oven to 375°.
2. Lightly spoon flour into a dry measuring cup, and level with a knife. Place flour in a large saucepan. Gradually add milk, stirring with a whisk until blended. Cook over medium heat 8 minutes, or until thick, stirring constantly. Add cheeses; cook 3 minutes or until cheeses melt, stirring frequently. Remove from heat; stir in macaroni and salt.
3. Spoon mixture into a 2-quart casserole coated with cooking spray. Combine crushed toasts and butter in a small bowl; stir until well blended. Sprinkle over macaroni mixture. Bake at 375° for 30 minutes or until bubbly. Yield: 8 servings (serving size: 1 cup).

CALORIES 350 (29% from fat); FAT 11.2g (sat 6.3g, mono 2.9g, poly 0.9g); PROTEIN 18g; CARB 42.4g; FIBER 2.1g; CHOL 32mg; IRON 1.9mg; SODIUM 497mg; CALC 306mg

The combination of fontina, Parmesan, Cheddar, and processed cheese packs a flavor punch. Fresh Parmesan and a good extrasharp Cheddar are essential.

Easy Meatless Manicotti

2 cups (8 ounces) shredded part-skim mozzarella cheese, divided
1 (16-ounce) carton fat-free cottage cheese
1 (10-ounce) package frozen chopped spinach, thawed, drained, and squeezed dry
¼ cup (1 ounce) grated fresh Parmesan cheese
1½ teaspoons dried oregano
¼ teaspoon salt
¼ teaspoon black pepper
1 (8-ounce) package manicotti (14 shells)
1 (26-ounce) jar fat-free tomato-basil pasta sauce
Cooking spray
1 cup water

1. Preheat oven to 375°.
2. Combine 1½ cups mozzarella, cottage cheese, and next 5 ingredients in a medium bowl. Spoon about 3 tablespoons cheese mixture into each uncooked manicotti. Pour half of pasta sauce into a 13 x 9–inch baking dish coated with cooking spray. Arrange stuffed shells in a single layer over sauce, and top with remaining sauce. Pour 1 cup water into dish. Sprinkle ½ cup mozzarella evenly over sauce. Cover tightly with foil. Bake at 375° for 1 hour or until shells are tender. Let stand 10 minutes before serving. Yield: 7 servings (serving size: 2 manicotti).

CALORIES 328 (25% from fat); FAT 9g (sat 4.8g, mono 2.2g, poly 0.5g); PROTEIN 23.8g; CARB 38.3g; FIBER 3.9g; CHOL 23mg; IRON 3mg; SODIUM 891mg; CALC 451mg

There's absolutely no shame in using jarred pasta sauce in your dishes. Pasta sauces on the supermarket shelves range from simple and inexpensive to exotic and pricey; it just depends on your needs. You can also purchase a plain sauce and enhance it at home with fresh herbs, spices, meats, and cheeses—then it's almost as if you made it from scratch. Use light or fat-free pasta sauce to save on calories, sodium, and fat in rich dishes like this manicotti.

Because the only preparation this casserole requires is assembly—no chopping or stovetop cooking—it's a great way to get the kids involved in the kitchen. The uncooked shells are easier to handle. If you have trouble stuffing them with a spoon, use a butter knife.

Grilled Vegetable Pasta Salad

Serrano chiles, whose name means "from the highlands," are believed to have originated in the foothills north of Puebla, Mexico. High in vitamin A and a good source of vitamin C and the B vitamins, the chiles have a slightly fruity flavor and a delayed bite. Their heat is somewhere between the milder jalapeño and the more intense habanero.

1 red bell pepper, halved and seeded
1 red onion, peeled and cut into 6 wedges
Cooking spray
1 (4-inch) portobello cap
¾ pound asparagus
½ tablespoon chopped serrano chile
3 garlic cloves, crushed
¼ teaspoon salt
1½ tablespoons red wine vinegar
1 tablespoon water
1 tablespoon fresh lemon juice
2 teaspoons extravirgin olive oil
2 teaspoons anchovy paste
4 cups cooked fusilli (about 8 ounces uncooked short twisted spaghetti)
¾ cup (3 ounces) crumbled feta cheese
½ cup chopped fresh basil
3 tablespoons chopped pitted kalamata olives

1. Prepare grill.
2. Coat bell pepper and onion with cooking spray; place on grill rack coated with cooking spray. Grill 15 minutes or until pepper is blackened, turning onion occasionally. Place pepper in a zip-top plastic bag; seal. Let stand 15 minutes. Coat mushroom cap and asparagus with cooking spray; place on grill rack, and grill 3 minutes on each side or until tender.
3. Chop onion into 1-inch pieces; place in a large bowl. Chop mushroom into 1-inch pieces; add to onion. Slice asparagus diagonally into 1½-inch pieces; add to onion mixture.
4. Combine chile, garlic, and salt in a mortar; mash to a paste with a pestle. Combine garlic paste, vinegar, and next 4 ingredients in a small bowl, stirring with a whisk.
5. Peel and slice pepper into ½-inch strips; add to onion mixture. Add chile mixture; toss well. Toss in pasta and remaining 3 ingredients. Yield: 4 servings (serving size: 2 cups).

CALORIES 364 (27% from fat); FAT 11.1g (sat 5g, mono 4.4g, poly 0.7g); PROTEIN 14.7g; CARB 53.1g; FIBER 4.3g; CHOL 27mg; IRON 3.2mg; SODIUM 985mg; CALC 198mg

Pack this robust pasta salad for a family picnic or serve it for an alfresco lunch. Toss the vegetables with the pasta when they're hot off the grill or after chilling.

Fusilli with Roasted Tomato Sauce

Both crushed and minced garlic enhance this delicious sauce. Crushed garlic releases mild flavor over a long period of time, which is why it's perfect to roast alongside the tomatoes. To crush garlic, mash the cloves with the flat side of a chef's knife. Sautéed minced garlic cooks with the sauce for more intense flavor. You can use a garlic press instead of mincing the garlic, but we don't recommend it because it can bruise the cloves and create a bitter taste.

2 tablespoons extravirgin olive oil, divided
6 large tomatoes (about 3½ pounds), cored, cut in half crosswise, and seeded
3 garlic cloves, crushed
1 teaspoon chopped fresh or ¼ teaspoon dried thyme
¾ teaspoon salt, divided
2 garlic cloves, minced
2½ tablespoons chopped fresh basil
¼ teaspoon black pepper
3½ cups hot cooked long fusilli (about 8 ounces uncooked twisted spaghetti)
¼ cup (1 ounce) shredded fresh Parmesan cheese
Basil sprigs (optional)

1. Preheat oven to 400°.
2. Brush a jelly-roll pan or shallow roasting pan with 1 tablespoon oil. Arrange tomatoes in a single layer, cut sides down, in pan. Arrange crushed garlic around tomatoes; sprinkle tomatoes with thyme and ¼ teaspoon salt.
3. Bake at 400° for 30 minutes; drain juices from pan. Bake an additional 30 minutes. Remove tomatoes from pan; cool slightly. Discard juice and crushed garlic. Peel and coarsely chop tomatoes.
4. Heat 1 tablespoon oil in a large nonstick skillet over medium-low heat. Add minced garlic, and cook 2 minutes, stirring frequently. Add chopped tomatoes and chopped basil, and cook 3 minutes or until thoroughly heated. Stir in ½ teaspoon salt and pepper. Add pasta, and toss to coat. Sprinkle with cheese; garnish with basil sprigs, if desired. Yield: 4 servings (serving size: about 1 cup pasta mixture and 1 tablespoon cheese).

CALORIES 347 (28% from fat); FAT 10.7g (sat 2.4g, mono 5.8g, poly 1.5g); PROTEIN 11.9g; CARB 54.1g; FIBER 6.6g; CHOL 5mg; IRON 3.7mg; SODIUM 591mg; CALC 121mg

Oven-roasting tomatoes with garlic and herbs boosts the flavor in this meatless sauce.

Red Bean Stew with Ditalini

Originally a sauce made from the fresh, wild basil that grows on the hills of Liguria, Italy, pesto is now a popular sauce used on more than just pasta. Made of garlic, basil, pine nuts, Parmesan or Romano cheese, and olive oil, it can be spread onto toasted bread, used in place of red sauce on pizzas, or blended into a soup, as it is here. As an added convenience, commercial pesto is available year-round from your local supermarket.

1 tablespoon olive oil
1½ cups presliced mushrooms
1 cup diced carrot
1½ cups water
¼ teaspoon black pepper
1 (15-ounce) can kidney beans, rinsed and drained
1 (14.5-ounce) can diced tomatoes, undrained
1 (14-ounce) can less-sodium beef broth
4 ounces uncooked ditalini (short tube-shaped pasta)
2 tablespoons commercial pesto (such as Alessi)
¼ cup (1 ounce) shredded fresh Parmesan cheese

1. Heat oil in a Dutch oven over medium-high heat. Add mushrooms and carrot; sauté 4 minutes. Stir in water and next 4 ingredients. Cover; bring to a boil. Stir in pasta; cook, uncovered, 11 minutes or until pasta is done. Stir in pesto; sprinkle each serving with cheese. Yield: 4 servings (serving size: 1½ cups stew and 1 tablespoon cheese).

CALORIES 324 (28% from fat); FAT 10.2g (sat 2.3g, mono 4.7g, poly 1.7g); PROTEIN 15.2g; CARB 43.7g; FIBER 10.4g; CHOL 6mg; IRON 3.1mg; SODIUM 560mg; CALC 150mg

This hearty stew is a one-dish meal in the truest sense. Add the uncooked ditalini straight to the pot—it cooks right along with the stew.

Sun-Dried Tomato-Tortellini Soup

Whether packed in oil or dry-packed, sun-dried tomatoes add vivid flavor and a healthy dose of lycopene to your cooking. To chop dry-packed tomatoes, coat a chef's knife with cooking spray; it will keep the tomatoes from sticking to the blade. There's no need to steep the tomatoes for this recipe; they rehydrate in the soup.

1½ teaspoons olive oil
  1 cup chopped onion
  1 cup (¼-inch-thick) slices
    carrot
  ⅔ cup chopped celery
  2 garlic cloves, minced
  5 cups fat-free, less-sodium
    chicken broth
  2 cups water
1¼ cups sun-dried tomato
    halves, packed without oil,
    chopped (about 3 ounces)
  ½ teaspoon dried basil
  ¼ teaspoon freshly ground
    black pepper
  1 bay leaf
  3 cups (about 12 ounces) fresh
    cheese tortellini
  1 cup chopped bok choy

1. Heat oil in a large Dutch oven over medium-high heat. Add onion, carrot, celery, and garlic; sauté 5 minutes. Add broth and next 5 ingredients; bring to a boil. Reduce heat; simmer 2 minutes. Add pasta and bok choy, and simmer 7 minutes or until pasta is done. Discard bay leaf. Yield: 6 servings (serving size: about 1½ cups).

CALORIES 256 (28% from fat); FAT 8g (sat 2.6g, mono 3.9g, poly 0.7g); PROTEIN 12.1g; CARB 33.9g; FIBER 3.9g; CHOL 25mg; IRON 1.1mg; SODIUM 681mg; CALC 47mg

Fix it in a flash—this filling soup comes together in about 20 minutes. And it tastes even better the next day.

Spaghetti and Meatballs

It's important to make meatballs that are similar in size so that they cook evenly. For 1-inch meatballs, pat the meat mixture into a 5-inch square about 1-inch thick. Cut into 1-inch cubes and gently shape into meatballs. Overmixing the meatballs can cause them to be tough and dry.

1 pound ground sirloin
¼ cup minced fresh onion
2 tablespoons dry breadcrumbs
¼ teaspoon garlic salt
¼ teaspoon black pepper
1 large egg white, lightly beaten
1 (25.5-ounce) jar fat-free tomato-and-basil pasta sauce, divided
Cooking spray
5 tablespoons chopped fresh basil
5 cups hot cooked spaghetti or vermicelli (about 8 ounces uncooked pasta)
5 tablespoons grated Parmesan cheese
Basil sprigs (optional)

1. Combine first 6 ingredients and 2 tablespoons pasta sauce in a medium bowl. Shape meat mixture into 25 (1-inch) meatballs. Place a large nonstick skillet over medium heat. Coat pan with cooking spray. Add meatballs, and cook 6 minutes, browning on all sides. Stir in remaining pasta sauce and chopped basil. Cover, reduce heat, and simmer 10 minutes or until meatballs are done, stirring occasionally. Serve meatballs over spaghetti; sprinkle with Parmesan cheese. Garnish with basil sprigs, if desired. Yield: 5 servings (serving size: 5 meatballs, ½ cup sauce, 1 cup pasta, and 1 tablespoon cheese).

CALORIES 476 (19% from fat); FAT 10g (sat 3.8g, mono 3.7g, poly 0.8g); PROTEIN 38.2g; CARB 42.8g; FIBER 4.9g; CHOL 78mg; IRON 5.5mg; SODIUM 651mg; CALC 217mg

Italian immigrant restaurateurs developed this dish at the beginning of the 20th century. Meatballs were added to spaghetti to adapt traditional Italian cuisine—mostly vegetables, legumes, and starches—to American tastes. Our quick-and-easy version tastes just like Grandma's.

Chili and Cheddar Farfalle Casserole

Chipotle chiles in adobo sauce are smoked jalapeño chile peppers that are canned with a sauce made of vinegar, tomato sauce, chiles, and herbs. The sauce is most often used as an ingredient in chili, soups, and sauces for medium heat and savory flavor. You can use the chiles, the sauce, or both in recipes.

1 (7-ounce) can chipotle chiles in adobo sauce
1 tablespoon butter
1 cup chopped red bell pepper
½ cup diced Canadian bacon (about 2 ounces)
1 cup thinly sliced green onions
2 tablespoons all-purpose flour
1 teaspoon chili powder
½ teaspoon salt
½ teaspoon ground cumin
2¼ cups 2% reduced-fat milk
2 cups (8 ounces) shredded reduced-fat sharp Cheddar cheese, divided
2 tablespoons chopped fresh cilantro
8 cups hot cooked farfalle (about 6 cups uncooked bow tie pasta) or other short pasta
Cooking spray

1. Preheat oven to 400°.
2. Remove 1 teaspoon adobo sauce and 1 chile from canned chiles; mince chile. Place remaining sauce and chiles in a zip-top plastic bag; freeze for another use.
3. Melt butter in a large Dutch oven over medium-high heat. Add bell pepper and bacon; sauté 4 minutes. Add onions; sauté 1 minute. Stir in adobo sauce, minced chile, flour, chili powder, salt, and cumin; cook 1 minute. Gradually add milk; cook until thick and bubbly (about 4 minutes), stirring constantly with a whisk. Remove from heat. Gradually add 1½ cups cheese and cilantro, stirring until cheese melts. Add pasta to pan; toss well.
4. Spoon pasta mixture into an 11 x 7–inch baking dish coated with cooking spray. Sprinkle ½ cup cheese over pasta mixture. Bake at 400° for 15 minutes or until browned. Yield: 6 servings (serving size: 1⅓ cups).

CALORIES 369 (30% from fat); FAT 12.4g (sat 7.4g, mono 1.6g, poly 1g); PROTEIN 23.2g; CARB 43g; FIBER 3.1g; CHOL 44mg; IRON 1.6mg; SODIUM 758mg; CALC 472mg

This casserole is one of those tried-and-true recipes that's perfect any night of the week. If you don't have farfalle, substitute ziti, rigatoni, or even macaroni.

Turkey Tetrazzini

Sherry is a fortified Spanish wine appreciated for its slightly nutty, apple flavor. Typically served in small glasses before a meal, it's also useful in the kitchen to perk up sauces, soups, and desserts. Don't be tempted to substitute cooking sherry for dry sherry; it can be very salty.

10 ounces uncooked vermicelli
2 teaspoons vegetable oil
1 pound turkey breast cutlets
¾ teaspoon onion powder, divided
½ teaspoon salt, divided
¼ teaspoon black pepper, divided
2 tablespoons dry sherry
2 (8-ounce) packages presliced mushrooms
¾ cup frozen green peas, thawed
¾ cup fat-free milk
⅔ cup fat-free sour cream
⅓ cup (about 1½ ounces) grated fresh Parmesan cheese
1 (10¾-ounce) can reduced-fat cream of chicken soup (such as Healthy Choice)
Cooking spray
⅓ cup dry breadcrumbs
2 tablespoons butter, melted

1. Preheat oven to 450°.
2. Cook pasta according to package directions, omitting salt and fat. Drain.
3. Heat oil in a large nonstick skillet over medium-high heat. Sprinkle turkey with ½ teaspoon onion powder, ¼ teaspoon salt, and ⅛ teaspoon pepper. Add turkey to pan; cook 2 minutes on each side or until done. Remove turkey from pan.
4. Add ¼ teaspoon onion powder, sherry, and mushrooms to pan. Cover mixture, and cook 4 minutes or until mushrooms are tender.
5. Combine peas and next 4 ingredients in a large bowl. Chop turkey. Add ¼ teaspoon salt, ⅛ teaspoon pepper, pasta, turkey, and mushroom mixture to soup mixture, tossing gently to combine. Spoon mixture into a 13 x 9–inch baking dish coated with cooking spray.
6. Combine breadcrumbs and butter in a small dish, tossing to combine. Sprinkle breadcrumb mixture over pasta mixture. Bake at 450° for 12 minutes or until bubbly and thoroughly heated. Yield: 6 servings (serving size: about 1⅔ cups).

CALORIES 459 (29% from fat); FAT 14.8g (sat 5.9g, mono 4.4g, poly 2.8g); PROTEIN 30.5g; CARB 48.1g; FIBER 3.1g; CHOL 69mg; IRON 4mg; SODIUM 716mg; CALC 199mg

By using just a few convenience products, such as presliced mushrooms, frozen peas, and canned soup, you can get made-from-scratch flavor fast. A splash of sherry, freshly grated Parmesan cheese, and a crunchy breadcrumb topping elevate everyday fare to new heights. Make this dish ahead and refrigerate. Bake just before you're ready to serve.

dinner tonight

Angel Hair with Herbed Goat Cheese and Grape Tomatoes

12 ounces uncooked angel hair
    pasta
  1 tablespoon olive oil
1½ teaspoons bottled minced
    garlic
  2 cups grape or cherry
    tomatoes, halved (about
    1 pint)
⅔ cup fat-free, less-sodium
    chicken broth
  6 tablespoons crumbled garlic
    and herb-flavored goat
    cheese
⅓ cup chopped fresh basil
¼ teaspoon salt
¼ teaspoon black pepper
Basil sprigs (optional)

1. Cook pasta according to package directions, omitting salt and fat. Drain; place in a large bowl, and keep warm.
2. While pasta cooks, heat oil in a large nonstick skillet over medium-high heat. Add garlic; sauté 30 seconds. Add tomatoes; cook 2 minutes, stirring frequently. Add broth; cook 1 minute. Remove from heat. Add goat cheese, basil, salt, and pepper to pasta; stir until well blended. Add tomato mixture to pasta mixture; toss gently to combine. Garnish with basil, if desired. Yield: 4 servings (serving size: about 1½ cups).

CALORIES 372 (28% from fat); FAT 11.5g (sat 4.9g, mono 4g, poly 0.6g); PROTEIN 16.5g; CARB 51.8g; FIBER 2.5g; CHOL 17mg; IRON 3.1mg; SODIUM 627mg; CALC 75mg

Once considered a specialty item, grape tomatoes are now mainstream, competing for shelf space with their large cousins—cherry tomatoes. Grape tomatoes, with their small size and sweet flavor, have become a popular low-calorie snack and salad ingredient. Oven-roasted whole, they make a simple and flavorful side dish. Halved and pan-sautéed, they add rich tomato flavor to pasta dishes.

Grape tomatoes bring the taste of summer to this pasta sauced with herbed goat cheese. Not only is this dish elegant, but it also comes together in about 20 minutes, making it perfect for any night of the week.

Cavatappi with Spinach, Beans, and Asiago Cheese

Quite popular in Italy, cannellini beans, also called white kidney or fazolia beans, are prized for their smooth texture and mellow nutty flavor. Because of their popularity, they're available year-round, either dried or canned. Dried cannellini beans must be soaked overnight and then boiled, but using canned beans can save time. Rinsing canned beans, as in this recipe, reduces the sodium by 40 percent.

8 cups coarsely chopped spinach leaves
4 cups hot cooked cavatappi (about 6 ounces uncooked spiral-shaped pasta)
½ cup (2 ounces) shredded Asiago cheese
2 tablespoons olive oil
¼ teaspoon salt
¼ teaspoon black pepper
2 garlic cloves, minced
1 (19-ounce) can cannellini beans or other white beans, rinsed and drained
Freshly ground black pepper (optional)

1. Combine first 8 ingredients in a large bowl; toss well. Sprinkle with freshly ground pepper, if desired. Yield: 4 servings (serving size: 2 cups).

CALORIES 401 (27% from fat); FAT 12g (sat 3.4g, mono 6.2g, poly 1.2g); PROTEIN 18.8g; CARB 54.7g; FIBER 6.7g; CHOL 10mg; IRON 6.4mg; SODIUM 464mg; CALC 306mg

If you toss the spinach and Asiago cheese with the pasta while it's still warm, the spinach will wilt and the cheese will soften. When this happens, the flavors blend and become more pungent.

Ziti with Chard

One of several leafy green vegetables referred to as "greens," Swiss chard offers an earthy, slightly salty flavor. It has fanlike leaves and thick, crunchy stalks in white, red, or yellow. A member of the same family as beets and spinach, chard can be used in most recipes that call for spinach. When buying chard, look for crisp leaves with no dark or moist patches, and avoid bunches with cracked or dried stems.

2 tablespoons olive oil
8 cups chopped Swiss chard
4 garlic cloves, minced
4 cups hot cooked ziti (about 8 ounces uncooked short tube-shaped pasta)
2 cups grape or cherry tomatoes, halved
¼ cup chopped pitted kalamata olives
2 tablespoons fresh lemon juice
¾ teaspoon kosher salt
½ teaspoon freshly ground black pepper
¼ cup (1 ounce) shaved fresh Romano cheese

1. Heat oil in a large nonstick skillet over medium-high heat. Add chard and garlic; sauté 2 minutes. Combine chard mixture, pasta, and next 5 ingredients, tossing well. Top with cheese. Yield: 4 servings (serving size: about 2 cups).

CALORIES 336 (28% from fat); FAT 10.5g (sat 2.4g, mono 6.2g, poly 0.8g); PROTEIN 12g; CARB 51g; FIBER 4.2g; CHOL 7mg; IRON 3.9mg; SODIUM 665mg; CALC 132mg

Swiss chard balances the intense combination of grape tomatoes, kalamata olives, and Romano cheese in this refreshing vegetarian dish.

Pasta with Roasted Butternut Squash and Shallots

Olive oil is not only better for you than most other oils, but it also has a fresh taste, an aromatic smell, and is very versatile. It can be used as a fat in cooking or as a condiment to add flavor. Here, it serves both purposes: It's used as a cooking fat to roast the squash and shallots, and it's tossed with the pasta to add a subtle hint of flavor.

3 cups (1-inch) cubed peeled butternut squash
1 tablespoon dark brown sugar
1½ tablespoons olive oil, divided
1 teaspoon salt
½ teaspoon black pepper
8 shallots, peeled and halved lengthwise (about ½ pound)
1 tablespoon chopped fresh or 1 teaspoon dried rubbed sage
4 ounces uncooked pappardelle (wide ribbon pasta) or fettuccine
¼ cup (1 ounce) shredded fresh Parmesan cheese

1. Preheat oven to 475°.
2. Combine squash, sugar, 2½ teaspoons oil, salt, pepper, and shallots in a jelly-roll pan, and toss well. Bake at 475° for 20 minutes or until tender, stirring occasionally. Stir in sage.
3. While squash mixture bakes, cook pasta according to package directions, omitting salt and fat. Drain. Place cooked pasta in a bowl. Add 2 teaspoons oil; toss well. Serve squash mixture over pasta. Sprinkle with cheese. Yield: 4 servings (serving size: ¾ cup pasta, ¾ cup squash mixture, and 1 tablespoon cheese).

CALORIES 248 (29% from fat); FAT 7.9g (sat 2g, mono 4.5g, poly 0.8g); PROTEIN 7.1g; CARB 39.4g; FIBER 5.2g; CHOL 5mg; IRON 1.4mg; SODIUM 713mg; CALC 137mg

Roasting enhances butternut squash, which blends nicely with the sage, shallots, and Parmesan. Use a sharp vegetable peeler to peel the butternut squash. It's easier to handle and less time consuming than using a knife. Serve this dish as a side to chicken or pork.

Scallops and Pasta with Pistachio-Parsley Pesto

The kernel, or inside seed, of a pistachio is ripe when the shell breaks open, causing an audible pop. Legend has it that lovers would meet under the pistachio trees' branches to listen for the sound, hoping for the promise of good luck. In addition to their unique flavor, pistachios also offer great nutritional benefits. A 1-ounce serving alone packs roughly 10% of the suggested daily value of fiber, vitamin B-6, and magnesium, making them chock-full of both good fortune and good health.

1 cup chopped fresh parsley
3 tablespoons coarsely chopped pistachios
1 teaspoon grated lemon rind
¼ teaspoon ground cumin
¼ teaspoon black pepper
⅛ teaspoon salt
⅛ teaspoon paprika
2 tablespoons fresh lemon juice
1¼ teaspoons olive oil
¾ pound sea scallops
¼ cup all-purpose flour
⅛ teaspoon salt
2 teaspoons butter
2 cups hot cooked angel hair (about 4 ounces uncooked pasta)
Freshly ground black pepper

1. Place first 9 ingredients in a food processor; process until smooth, scraping sides of processor bowl occasionally.
2. Combine scallops, flour, and ⅛ teaspoon salt in large zip-top plastic bag; seal and shake to coat.
3. Heat butter in nonstick skillet over medium-high heat. Add scallops; cook 3½ minutes on each side or until scallops are done.
4. Combine pesto mixture and pasta in a large bowl, tossing well. Arrange pasta on each plate, and place scallops on top of pasta. Sprinkle with pepper. Yield: 2 servings (serving size: 1 cup pasta and about 5 ounces scallops).

CALORIES 554 (25% from fat); FAT 15.2g (sat 3.9g, mono 6.4g, poly 3.5g); PROTEIN 41.4g; CARB 64.3g; FIBER 5g; CHOL 66mg; IRON 5.4mg; SODIUM 614mg; CALC 117mg

Make the pesto up to two days ahead; cover and chill. Be sure to buy sea scallops, not bay scallops. Sea scallops are bigger than bay scallops (about 1½ inches in diameter compared to about ½ inch in diameter).

Pork and Fennel Ragù

Native to the Mediterranean region and a licorice-flavored member of the parsley family, fennel is one of Italy's most popular vegetables. Its culinary versatility is a plus; the entire plant is edible and can take the place of celery in soups and stews. When shopping for fennel, look for small, heavy, white bulbs that are firm and free of cracks, browning, or moist areas. The stalks should be crisp, with feathery, bright green fronds.

Cooking spray
  1 cup finely chopped onion
  1 cup finely chopped fennel bulb
  2 garlic cloves, minced
  1 tablespoon fennel seeds
  2 teaspoons sugar
  1 teaspoon dried oregano
  ½ teaspoon salt
  ½ teaspoon crushed red pepper
  ¼ teaspoon ground red pepper
  ¼ teaspoon freshly ground black pepper
  8 ounces lean ground pork
  2 cups chopped tomato
  ½ cup fat-free, less-sodium chicken broth
  4 cups hot cooked rigatoni (about 8 ounces uncooked pasta)
Fennel fronds (optional)

1. Heat a large nonstick skillet over medium-high heat. Coat pan with cooking spray. Add onion, chopped fennel, and garlic; sauté 5 minutes. Add fennel seeds and next 7 ingredients, stirring to combine; sauté 3 minutes.

2. Add tomato and broth; bring to a boil. Reduce heat, and simmer 15 minutes, stirring occasionally. Serve over pasta. Garnish with fennel fronds, if desired. Yield: 4 servings (serving size: 1 cup ragù and 1 cup pasta).

CALORIES 408 (30% from fat); FAT 13.7g (sat 4.7g, mono 5.7g, poly 1.6g); PROTEIN 18.6g; CARB 52.8g; FIBER 5g; CHOL 41mg; IRON 3.5mg; SODIUM 405mg; CALC 64mg

With onions, fennel, garlic, and oregano, this traditional ragù, or meat sauce, is reminiscent of Italian sausage.

Penne with Sausage, Eggplant, and Feta

Eggplants come in an assortment of colors, shapes, and sizes, and they have virtually no fat. An eggplant is mostly water, with only 13 calories per ½ cup. With its colorful, tough skin and spongy flesh, it's exceptionally versatile and mixes well with meats, cheeses, and all sorts of vegetables. The most common eggplant is the large, dark-purple American eggplant that can be found in supermarkets throughout the year. Look for eggplants that have smooth, shiny skin and are firm but slightly springy. Store them in a cool place, and use them within 2 days.

4½ cups cubed peeled eggplant (about 1 pound)
½ pound bulk pork breakfast sausage
4 garlic cloves, minced
2 tablespoons tomato paste
1 teaspoon dried oregano
¼ teaspoon freshly ground black pepper
1 (14.5-ounce) can diced tomatoes, undrained
6 cups hot cooked penne (about 10 ounces uncooked tube-shaped pasta)
½ cup (2 ounces) crumbled feta cheese
¼ cup chopped fresh parsley

1. Cook eggplant, sausage, and garlic in a large nonstick skillet over medium-high heat 5 minutes or until sausage is browned and eggplant is tender. Add tomato paste and next 3 ingredients; cook over medium heat 5 minutes, stirring occasionally.
2. Place pasta in a large bowl. Add tomato mixture, cheese, and parsley; toss well. Yield: 4 servings (serving size: 2 cups).

CALORIES 535 (32% from fat); FAT 18.9g (sat 7.6g, mono 7.5g, poly 2.1g); PROTEIN 25.5g; CARB 67.5g; FIBER 4.6g; CHOL 57mg; IRON 4.5mg; SODIUM 884mg; CALC 141mg

Meaty breakfast sausage, earthy eggplant, and zesty feta complement each other in this hearty pasta dish. Buy precrumbled feta cheese to save time.

Pasta with Prosciutto and Peas

Prosciutto, also known as Parma ham, is dry-cured ham. A pork leg is rubbed with salt and refrigerated for several weeks. Once the salt penetrates the bone, it's washed away and the pork is left to age for about 14 to 24 months in a cool place. The aging process gives this ham its distinct flavor. Prosciutto is typically sliced thin and eaten raw or lightly cooked. Domestic prosciutto is fine for flavoring sauces, soups, and stews. But when you're looking for the gold, go for *prosciutto di Parma*, denoting that it's from the Parma area of Italy; it's considered the ultimate indulgence.

Cooking spray
3 ounces very thin slices prosciutto, chopped
3 tablespoons extravirgin olive oil
2 garlic cloves, thinly sliced
6 cups hot cooked fusilli (about 12 ounces uncooked short twisted spaghetti)
1 cup (4 ounces) shaved Parmigiano-Reggiano cheese
⅓ cup chopped fresh parsley
1 tablespoon fresh lemon juice
½ teaspoon kosher salt
½ teaspoon freshly ground black pepper
1 (10-ounce) package frozen peas, cooked and drained

1. Heat a large nonstick skillet over medium heat. Coat pan with cooking spray. Add prosciutto; cook 3 minutes or until lightly browned. Remove from pan. Add oil and garlic to pan; cook 1 minute or until garlic begins to brown. Combine prosciutto, oil mixture, pasta, and remaining ingredients in a large bowl; toss to coat. Yield: 8 servings (serving size: 1 cup).

CALORIES 312 (31% from fat); FAT 10.6g (sat 3.5g, mono 5.4g, poly 1.1g); PROTEIN 14.9g; CARB 37.8g; FIBER 1.2g; CHOL 16mg; IRON 2.7mg; SODIUM 554mg; CALC 189mg

This simple pasta toss is all about quality ingredients—Parmigiano-Reggiano cheese, prosciutto, extravirgin olive oil, fresh parsley, and freshly ground black pepper. To save time, add the frozen peas to the pasta during the last 3 minutes of cook time and drain.

Chicken and Chucka Soba with Peanut Sauce

Japanese curly noodles, made from wheat flour, are long and wavy with a delicate texture and mild flavor. Their Japanese name, chucka soba, translates to "Chinese noodle." Parboiled chucka soba are often used to make yakisoba, or "fried noodles." However they're used, these noodles are a staple in quick-and-easy cuisine. Find them in the Asian section of your supermarket.

5 ounces uncooked Japanese curly noodles (chucka soba)
2 teaspoons dark sesame oil, divided
1 pound chicken breast tenders
1½ cups red bell pepper strips
½ cup fat-free, less-sodium chicken broth
⅓ cup hoisin sauce
¼ cup creamy peanut butter
2 tablespoons rice vinegar
2 tablespoons ketchup
¼ teaspoon crushed red pepper
1 tablespoon bottled ground fresh ginger (such as Spice World)
1 teaspoon bottled minced garlic
½ cup chopped green onions, divided

1. Cook noodles according to package directions; drain.
2. Heat 1 teaspoon oil in a large nonstick skillet over medium-high heat. Add chicken; sauté 4 minutes. Add bell pepper; sauté 3 minutes. Remove from heat. Combine chicken mixture and noodles in a large bowl.
3. Combine broth and next 5 ingredients in a bowl; stir well with a whisk.
4. Heat 1 teaspoon oil in pan over medium heat. Add ginger and garlic; cook 15 seconds. Stir in broth mixture, and cook 30 seconds, stirring constantly. Add broth mixture and ¼ cup green onions to noodle mixture; toss well. Sprinkle with ¼ cup green onions. Yield: 5 servings (serving size: 1 cup).

CALORIES 353 (28% from fat); FAT 10.9g (sat 2g, mono 4.3g, poly 3.1g); PROTEIN 28.5g; CARB 36g; FIBER 2.3g; CHOL 53mg; IRON 1.5mg; SODIUM 663mg; CALC 21mg

This dish is great served at room temperature or cold; add a touch of warm water to loosen the noodles if serving cold. Serve with steamed broccoli for a complete meal.

Pan-Seared Chicken with Artichokes and Pasta

Most pastas are interchangeable if you use a variety that is similar to the shape and size specified in the recipe. Here, the twists, turns, and ridges of cavatappi and fusilli are perfect for trapping the many flavors in this chunky sauce.

1 (6-ounce) jar marinated artichoke heart quarters, undrained
8 skinless, boneless chicken thighs (about 1½ pounds)
¼ teaspoon salt
¼ teaspoon black pepper
Cooking spray
½ cup sliced green onions
1 garlic clove, minced
½ cup dry white wine
4 cups hot cooked cavatappi (about 2½ cups uncooked spiral tube-shaped pasta) or fusilli (short twisted spaghetti)
1 tablespoon chopped pitted kalamata olives
1 (14.5-ounce) canned diced tomatoes, drained
2 tablespoons shredded fresh Parmesan cheese

1. Drain artichokes in a colander over a bowl, reserving marinade.
2. Sprinkle chicken with salt and pepper; coat with cooking spray. Heat a large nonstick skillet over medium-high heat. Add chicken; sauté 3 minutes on each side. Add onions and garlic; sauté 1 minute. Stir in reserved artichoke marinade and wine, scraping pan to loosen browned bits. Bring to a boil; reduce heat, and stir in artichokes, pasta, olives, and tomatoes. Cook 2 minutes or until thoroughly heated. Sprinkle with cheese. Yield: 4 servings (serving size: 2 thighs and about 1¾ cups pasta mixture).

CALORIES 436 (29% from fat); FAT 14g (sat 3.4g, mono 4.6g, poly 4.4g); PROTEIN 34.4g; CARB 39g; FIBER 1.9g; CHOL 115mg; IRON 3.9mg; SODIUM 594mg; CALC 96mg

Since you cook everything in one pan, the larger the pan, the better. Slightly undercook the cavatappi; it will finish cooking when you add it to the chicken mixture.

casual entertaining

Green-Chile Ravioli

Ravioli:
- 1 cup (4 ounces) preshredded reduced-fat Mexican blend cheese
- ¼ cup minced green onions
- ½ teaspoon black pepper
- 1 (4.5-ounce) can chopped green chiles, undrained
- 1 large egg white
- 16 wonton wrappers
- 1 teaspoon cornstarch
- Cooking spray
- ⅓ cup fat-free, less-sodium chicken broth

Sauce:
- ½ cup minced fresh cilantro
- 2 tablespoons balsamic vinegar
- 2 (14.5-ounce) cans diced tomatoes, drained
- 1 (15-ounce) can black beans, rinsed and drained
- 1 teaspoon olive oil

Wonton wrappers are a short-cut ingredient to homemade ravioli. Though Chinese in origin, wonton wrappers are similar to fresh pasta dough in texture, flavor, and nutritional value. They can be used to wrap foods of any cuisine. Look for wonton wrappers in the refrigerated case of the supermarket produce section.

1. To prepare ravioli, combine first 5 ingredients in a bowl. Working with 1 wonton wrapper at a time (cover remaining wrappers with a damp towel to keep from drying), spoon about 1 tablespoon green chile mixture into center of wrapper. Brush edges of wrapper with water; bring 2 opposite corners together. Press edges together firmly with fingers, forming a triangle. Place ravioli on a large baking sheet sprinkled with cornstarch. Heat a large nonstick skillet over medium-high heat. Coat pan with cooking spray. Add ravioli; cook 2 to 3 minutes on each side or until lightly browned. Add broth; cook, covered, 1 to 2 minutes. Remove ravioli with a slotted spoon, and keep warm.

2. To prepare sauce, combine cilantro, vinegar, tomatoes, beans, and oil in a large saucepan over medium-high heat. Cook 5 minutes or until thoroughly heated. Spoon sauce over ravioli. Yield: 4 servings (serving size: 4 ravioli and ¾ cup sauce).

CALORIES 271 (28% from fat); FAT 8.3g (sat 3.2g, mono 0.9g, poly 0.4g); PROTEIN 16.4g; CARB 41g; FIBER 7.3g; CHOL 23mg; IRON 2.9mg; SODIUM 892mg; CALC 340mg

These nontraditional ravioli with Tex-Mex flair look beautiful on a plate, making this easy entrée an ideal choice for company.

Pasta and Grilled Vegetables with Goat Cheese

Radicchio is an Italian leaf vegetable whose varieties are named after the Italian regions where they originate. In Italy, where the vegetable is quite popular, radicchio is normally eaten grilled with olive oil. It has a bitter, somewhat spicy taste that mellows when roasted or grilled, as it is here.

1 large zucchini, quartered lengthwise (about 8 ounces)
1 red bell pepper, cut into 4 wedges
1 leek, trimmed and halved
1 (14-ounce) can artichoke hearts, drained
1 head radicchio, quartered
½ teaspoon salt, divided
¼ teaspoon freshly ground black pepper
2 garlic cloves, minced
Cooking spray
4 cups hot cooked rotini (about 4 cups uncooked corkscrew pasta)
1 cup grape or cherry tomatoes
¾ cup (3 ounces) crumbled goat cheese
2 tablespoons thinly sliced fresh basil

1. Prepare grill.
2. Arrange first 5 ingredients in a single layer on a jelly-roll pan; sprinkle evenly with ¼ teaspoon salt, black pepper, and garlic. Lightly coat vegetables with cooking spray. Place vegetables on grill rack; grill 3 minutes on each side or until browned and tender. Remove vegetables to a cutting board; chop into bite-sized pieces.
3. Place pasta in a large bowl; sprinkle with ¼ teaspoon salt, tossing well. Stir in grilled vegetables and tomatoes; sprinkle each serving with cheese and basil. Yield: 4 servings (serving size: 2½ cups pasta mixture, 3 tablespoons cheese, and 1½ teaspoons basil).

CALORIES 327 (16% from fat); FAT 5.8g (sat 3.5g, mono 1g, poly 0.3g); PROTEIN 14g; CARB 56.3g; FIBER 3.4g; CHOL 19mg; IRON 3.8mg; SODIUM 682mg; CALC 149mg

This vibrant vegetable entrée is light and delicious. To ensure even grilling, cut the vegetables into large, similar-sized pieces. After cooking, chop into bite-sized pieces. You can substitute yellow squash for zucchini.

Pasta with Mushrooms and Pumpkin-Gorgonzola Sauce

While fresh pumpkin is only available seasonally, canned pumpkin is stocked year-round at your local super-market and offers the same nutritional value as fresh. Use canned pumpkin to enhance the flavor or color of a particular sauce or recipe. Here, it's added to a mush-room mixture and then tossed with fresh pasta for a savory twist.

1 pound uncooked pennette (small penne)
1 tablespoon olive oil
5 cups thinly sliced shiitake mushroom caps (about ¾ pound whole mushrooms)
4 cups vertically sliced onion
4 garlic cloves, minced
1 teaspoon chopped fresh sage
1 (12-ounce) can evaporated milk
1½ tablespoons cornstarch
1½ tablespoons cold water
½ cup (2 ounces) crumbled Gorgonzola cheese
½ cup canned pumpkin
1 teaspoon salt
½ teaspoon freshly ground black pepper
⅛ teaspoon grated whole nutmeg
Sage sprigs (optional)

1. Cook pasta according to package directions, omitting salt and fat. Drain. Keep pasta warm.
2. Heat oil in a Dutch oven over medium-high heat. Add mushrooms, onion, and garlic; cover and cook 3 minutes. Uncover and cook 5 minutes or until tender, stirring occasionally.
3. Combine chopped sage and milk in a medium saucepan over medium heat. Bring to a simmer. Combine cornstarch and water, stirring with a whisk. Add cornstarch mixture and cheese to milk mixture, stirring with a whisk. Cook 2 minutes or until thick and smooth, stirring constantly. Remove from heat; stir in pumpkin, salt, pepper, and nutmeg.
4. Add pasta and pumpkin mixture to mushroom mixture; toss well to combine. Garnish with sage sprigs, if desired. Yield: 6 servings (serving size: 1½ cups).

CALORIES 462 (13% from fat); FAT 6.5g (sat 2.8g, mono 1.7g, poly 0.4g); PROTEIN 19.9g; CARB 83.1g; FIBER 7.3g; CHOL 11mg; IRON 3.7mg; SODIUM 636mg; CALC 265mg

Any short pasta will work in this dish. For the sauce, we recommend our favorite brand of cheese: Saladena Gorgonzola; when melted into the other ingredients, it yields a luscious consistency.

Four-Cheese Stuffed Shells with Smoky Marinara

Getting the filling into stuffed shells or manicotti can be a challenge. Using a heavy-duty zip-top plastic bag as a pastry bag makes it easier. Simply spoon the filling into the plastic bag, squeeze out the air, snip a 1-inch hole in one corner of the bag, and pipe the filling into the shells. Snip a small hole to start with; you can always make it bigger.

1 pound uncooked jumbo shell pasta (40 shells)
Cooking spray
1 (12-ounce) carton 1% low-fat cottage cheese
1 (15-ounce) carton ricotta cheese
1 cup (4 ounces) shredded Asiago cheese
¾ cup (3 ounces) grated fresh Parmesan cheese
2 tablespoons chopped fresh chives
2 tablespoons chopped fresh parsley
¼ teaspoon black pepper
¼ teaspoon salt
1 (10-ounce) package frozen chopped spinach, thawed, drained, and squeezed dry
6 cups Smoky Marinara (recipe on page 141), divided
1 cup (4 ounces) shredded part-skim mozzarella cheese, divided
Parsley sprigs (optional)

1. Cook pasta according to package directions, omitting salt and fat. Drain and set aside.

2. Preheat oven to 375°.

3. Coat 2 (13 x 9–inch) baking dishes with cooking spray; set aside.

4. Place cottage cheese and ricotta cheese in a food processor; process until smooth. Combine cottage cheese mixture, Asiago, and next 6 ingredients.

5. Spoon or pipe 1 tablespoon cheese mixture into each shell. Arrange half of stuffed shells, seam sides up, in one prepared dish. Pour 3 cups Smoky Marinara over stuffed shells. Sprinkle with ½ cup mozzarella. Repeat procedure with remaining stuffed shells, 3 cups Smoky Marinara, and ½ cup mozzarella in remaining prepared dish.

6. Cover with foil. Bake at 375° for 30 minutes or until thoroughly heated. Garnish with parsley, if desired. Yield: 2 casseroles, 5 servings per dish (serving size: 4 stuffed shells and about ½ cup Smoky Marinara).

To freeze unbaked casserole: Prepare through Step 5. Cover with plastic wrap, pressing to remove as much air as possible. Wrap with heavy-duty foil. Store in freezer up to two months.

To prepare frozen unbaked casserole: Preheat oven to 375°. Remove foil; reserve foil. Remove plastic wrap; discard wrap. Cover frozen casserole with reserved foil; bake at 375° for 1 hour and 10 minutes or until shells are thoroughly heated.

CALORIES 470 (30% from fat); FAT 15.7g (sat 8.8g, mono 4.7g, poly 0.9g); PROTEIN 28.3g; CARB 52.7g; FIBER 5.3g; CHOL 47mg; IRON 3.8mg; SODIUM 916mg; CALC 508mg

Creamy Gruyère and Shrimp Orecchiette

Orecchiette plumps up to nearly twice its size once cooked, and its shape is perfect for holding bits of soup or chunky pasta sauce. One side of the pasta is usually rougher than the other, ideal for capturing creamy sauces, like the one in this recipe.

8 ounces uncooked orecchiette pasta ("little ears" pasta)
¼ cup all-purpose flour
½ teaspoon salt
2 cups 2% reduced-fat milk
1¼ cups (5 ounces) shredded Gruyère cheese, divided
1 tablespoon butter
1½ pounds large shrimp, peeled and deveined
3 garlic cloves, minced
2 tablespoons dry white wine
¼ teaspoon ground red pepper
2 cups frozen green peas, thawed
Cooking spray
Parsley sprigs (optional)

1. Preheat oven to 375°.

2. Cook pasta according to package directions, omitting salt and fat. Drain well.

3. Combine flour and salt in a Dutch oven over medium heat. Gradually add milk, stirring constantly with a whisk; bring to a boil. Cook 1 minute or until slightly thick, stirring constantly with a whisk. Remove from heat. Stir in ¾ cup cheese, stirring until melted.

4. Heat butter in a large nonstick skillet over medium-high heat. Add shrimp and garlic, and sauté 3 minutes. Stir in wine and pepper, and cook 1 minute or until shrimp are done.

5. Add pasta, shrimp mixture, and peas to cheese mixture, tossing well to combine. Spoon pasta mixture into a 13 x 9–inch baking dish lightly coated with cooking spray; sprinkle evenly with ½ cup cheese. Bake at 375° for 20 minutes or until cheese melts and begins to brown. Garnish with parsley, if desired. Serve immediately. Yield: 6 servings.

CALORIES 459 (27% from fat); FAT 13.8g (sat 7.1g, mono 3.7g, poly 1.6g); PROTEIN 39.6g; CARB 41.2g; FIBER 2.5g; CHOL 210mg; IRON 4.1mg; SODIUM 535mg; CALC 415mg

Gruyère has a nutty, slightly sweet flavor; Swiss cheese makes a fine substitute. You can use chopped cooked chicken in place of the shrimp.

Shrimp, Tomato, and Basil Linguine with Warm Goat Cheese Rounds

The double-toasted bread-crumbs are a crunchy con-trast to the soft center of the goat cheese rounds. Pulse the bread in a food processor until the crumbs reach the desired size.

1 (1-ounce) slice white bread
1 (4-ounce) package log-shaped goat cheese
1 tablespoon olive oil
1 cup coarsely chopped onion
2 garlic cloves, minced
2½ cups chopped seeded peeled plum tomatoes (about 1½ pounds)
¼ cup water
1½ teaspoons sugar
¾ teaspoon crushed red pepper
½ pound medium shrimp, peeled and deveined
½ teaspoon salt
6 cups hot cooked linguine (about 12 ounces uncooked pasta)
½ cup thinly sliced fresh basil
Basil sprigs (optional)

1. Preheat oven to 400°.
2. Place bread in a food processor; pulse 10 times or until coarse crumbs measure ½ cup. Sprinkle breadcrumbs on a baking sheet; bake at 400° for 2½ minutes or until golden brown. Transfer to a shallow plate; cool completely. Slice goat cheese crosswise into 4 rounds. Press both sides of each round into breadcrumbs. Arrange in a single layer on a baking sheet; chill.
3. While goat cheese rounds chill, heat oil in a large non-stick skillet over medium-high heat. Add onion and garlic; sauté 5 minutes. Stir in chopped tomato, water, sugar, and pepper; cook mixture 15 minutes, stirring occasionally. Add shrimp and salt; cook 4 minutes or until shrimp are done. Remove from heat. Cover; keep warm.
4. Bake cheese rounds at 400° for 10 minutes or until soft but still holding their shape.
5. Add pasta and ½ cup basil to tomato mixture; toss to combine. Place pasta mixture into each of 4 bowls; top with goat cheese rounds. Garnish with basil sprigs, if desired. Yield: 4 servings (serving size: about 2 cups pasta mixture and 1 goat cheese round).

CALORIES 461 (28% from fat); FAT 14.3g (sat 6.7g, mono 4.8g, poly 1.4g); PROTEIN 24.5g; CARB 58.9g; FIBER 4.1g; CHOL 87mg; IRON 4.8mg; SODIUM 562mg; CALC 148mg

Just a little sugar and red pepper add a sweet-hot note to this dish and complement the acidity of the goat cheese. Prepare the goat cheese rounds a day ahead, and refrigerate to make this recipe extra-easy.

Fettuccine with Shrimp and Portobellos

Portobello mushrooms are listed among the top exotic mushroom sales in the United States. Known for its flying saucer–like disk, the portobello is firm, meaty, and intensely flavored. When choosing portobellos, be sure to check under the cap and avoid selecting those with flattened gills. Before sautéing porto-bellos, use a spoon to remove the dark-colored gills; this will prevent the mushrooms from turning black.

8 ounces uncooked fettuccine
1 (4-inch) portobello mushroom cap (about 5 ounces)
1 tablespoon olive oil
1 cup finely chopped onion
¼ cup chopped fresh flat-leaf parsley
¼ teaspoon salt
1 garlic clove, minced
1 cup fat-free, less-sodium chicken broth
¼ cup dry white wine
¾ pound large shrimp, peeled and deveined
½ cup (2 ounces) shredded Asiago cheese
1 tablespoon chopped fresh chives

1. Cook pasta according to package directions, omitting salt and fat. Drain and rinse under cold water. Drain.
2. Remove brown gills from underside of mushroom cap using a spoon; discard gills. Cut cap into thin slices. Cut slices in half crosswise.
3. Heat olive oil in a large saucepan over medium-high heat. Add mushroom, onion, parsley, salt, and garlic; sauté 4 minutes or until mushroom releases moisture, stirring frequently. Stir in broth, wine, and shrimp; bring to a boil. Add pasta, and cook 3 minutes or until shrimp are done, tossing to combine. Place shrimp mixture in each of 4 bowls. Sprinkle each serving with cheese and chives. Yield: 4 servings (serving size: 1¾ cups shrimp mixture, 2 tablespoons cheese, and about 1 teaspoon chives).

CALORIES 384 (21% from fat); FAT 9.1g (sat 3.3g, mono 2.7g, poly 0.9g); PROTEIN 23.8g; CARB 48.9g; FIBER 2.8g; CHOL 114mg; IRON 4.5mg; SODIUM 540mg; CALC 156mg

Serve supper in a bowl with toasted bread to soak up the flavorful liquid created by the mushrooms, wine, and chicken broth.

Creamy Fettuccine with Shrimp and Bacon

Green peas add fiber, color, and a slightly sweet snap to each bite of this creamy dish. Buying the peas frozen saves time and allows you to enjoy their fresh flavor year-round. A quick rinse under cold running water is all that's needed to thaw the frozen peas. Of course, if you happen to find some freshly shelled peas, feel free to substitute them for the frozen peas.

1 pound uncooked fettuccine
2 bacon slices (uncooked)
1 pound large shrimp, peeled and deveined
1 garlic clove, minced
1½ cups frozen green peas, thawed
1 cup shredded carrot
2 cups 2% reduced-fat milk
2 tablespoons all-purpose flour
½ teaspoon salt
½ teaspoon freshly ground black pepper
1 cup (4 ounces) grated Parmesan cheese
½ cup chopped fresh flat-leaf parsley, divided

1. Cook pasta according to package directions, omitting salt and fat. Drain well; keep warm.
2. Cook bacon in a large nonstick skillet over medium-high heat 6 minutes or until crisp. Remove bacon from pan, reserving 1 tablespoon drippings in pan. Crumble bacon; set aside.
3. Add shrimp and garlic to pan; sauté over medium-high heat 2 minutes. Add peas and carrot; cook 2 minutes or just until shrimp are done. Transfer shrimp mixture to a large bowl; keep warm.
4. Combine milk, flour, salt, and pepper, stirring with a whisk. Add milk mixture to pan; cook over medium heat 3 minutes or until thickened and bubbly, stirring constantly with a whisk. Remove pan from heat; add cheese, stirring until blended. Add milk mixture to shrimp mixture, and stir until combined. Add pasta and ¼ cup parsley, tossing gently to coat. Transfer pasta mixture to a platter, or place on each of 8 plates; sprinkle evenly with ¼ cup parsley and evenly crumbled bacon. Serve immediately. Yield: 8 servings (serving size: about 1¼ cups pasta mixture).

CALORIES 382 (18% from fat); FAT 7.7g (sat 3.7g, mono 1.2g, poly 0.5g); PROTEIN 25g; CARB 52.9g; FIBER 3.6g; CHOL 101mg; IRON 4.1mg; SODIUM 505mg; CALC 218mg

Whisking a couple tablespoons of flour into the milk achieves a texture in the sauce similar to that of cream. A little bit of bacon and drippings contribute smokiness and richness.

Squash-Stuffed Cannelloni with Roasted-Shallot Sauce

Shallots differ from onions in that many varieties produce a cluster of several bulbs to a plant. Shallots also have finer layers and contain less water. Because of the low water content, their flavor is more concentrated than that of onions. They can burn and toughen easily, so use caution when sautéing. When peeling a shallot, remove a couple of the outer layers along with the peel. You might need an extra shallot to make up for the discarded layers, but this method is a lot faster than removing only the thin peel.

Filling:
10 cups (½-inch) cubed peeled butternut squash
¼ cup chopped shallots
2 tablespoons chopped fresh sage
Cooking spray
1 tablespoon butter, melted
½ cup fat-free sour cream
¼ cup half-and-half
¼ teaspoon salt
¼ teaspoon freshly ground black pepper

Sauce:
3 slices applewood smoked bacon, chopped
½ pound shallots, peeled and halved
2 garlic cloves, crushed
½ cup dry white wine
1 (14-ounce) can fat-free, less-sodium chicken broth
2 tablespoons half-and-half
¼ teaspoon salt
¼ teaspoon freshly ground black pepper

Remaining ingredients:
16 cooked lasagna noodles
¾ cup (3 ounces) shredded fontina cheese
¼ cup chopped blanched hazelnuts, toasted
Sage leaves (optional)

1. Preheat oven to 400°.

2. To prepare filling, combine first 3 ingredients in a bowl. Place mixture on a jelly-roll pan coated with cooking spray. Drizzle with butter; toss to coat. Bake at 400° for 25 minutes or until lightly browned, stirring occasionally. Place squash mixture in a large bowl; mash with a potato masher. Stir in sour cream and next 3 ingredients.

3. To prepare sauce, cook bacon in an ovenproof Dutch oven over medium-high heat until crisp. Remove bacon from pan, reserving 2 teaspoons drippings in pan; set bacon aside. Add halved shallots and garlic to drippings in pan; sauté 5 minutes or until browned. Bake at 400° for 25 minutes, stirring occasionally. Place pan on stovetop over medium-high heat. Add wine, scraping pan to loosen browned bits. Add broth; bring to a boil. Reduce heat; simmer 5 minutes. Remove from heat; stir in 2 tablespoons half-and-half, ¼ teaspoon salt, and ¼ teaspoon pepper.

4. Spread ¼ cup filling over each noodle, leaving a ½-inch border on each short end. Beginning with a short end, roll up noodles jelly-roll fashion. Place rolls, seam sides down, in a 13 x 9–inch baking pan coated with cooking spray. Pour sauce over noodles; sprinkle evenly with cheese. Bake at 400° for 25 minutes or until cheese is golden. Sprinkle with bacon and hazelnuts. Yield: 8 servings (serving size: 2 cannelloni).

CALORIES 349 (29% from fat); FAT 11.4g (sat 5g, mono 4.5g, poly 1g); PROTEIN 12.2g; CARB 51.8g; FIBER 7.8g; CHOL 26mg; IRON 3mg; SODIUM 414mg; CALC 206mg

Prepare the filling up to one day in advance. You'll need about 4 pounds butternut squash to get 10 cups. For a vegetarian version, use vegetable broth in place of chicken broth; sauté the shallots and garlic in oil, omitting the bacon.

Curried Chicken Penne with Fresh Mango Chutney

A mango can be tricky to cut because of the large flat seed that clings to the flesh. To cut around the seed, hold the mango vertically on a cutting board. Slice the fruit lengthwise on each side of the flat seed. (You can't tell what side of the seed is flat from the outside, so if you hit the seed, turn the fruit a quarter turn and start again.) Holding one mango half in the palm of your hand, score the pulp in square cross-sections, slicing to, but not through, the skin. Turn the mango half inside out, and cut the chunks from the skin.

Chutney:
  2 cups diced peeled ripe
    mango (about 2 mangoes)
  1 cup finely chopped onion
  ½ cup water
  2 tablespoons brown sugar
  1 tablespoon curry powder
  1 tablespoon fresh lime juice
  ½ teaspoon black pepper
  ½ teaspoon chopped peeled
    fresh ginger
  ¼ teaspoon salt

Chicken:
  1 teaspoon olive oil
  2 garlic cloves, minced
  1 pound skinless, boneless
    chicken breast, cut into
    1-inch pieces
  1 cup light coconut milk
  2 tablespoons sugar
  1½ teaspoons red curry paste
  1 to 2 teaspoons Thai fish
    sauce
  1 teaspoon salt
  2 cups broccoli florets
  2 cups cauliflower florets
  4 cups hot cooked penne
    rigate (about 2 cups
    uncooked tube-shaped
    pasta)
  2 tablespoons chopped green
    onions (optional)

1. To prepare chutney, combine first 9 ingredients in a medium saucepan; bring to a boil. Reduce heat, and simmer 15 minutes or until most of liquid evaporates and mixture is thick, stirring occasionally.

2. To prepare chicken, heat oil in a large nonstick skillet over medium-high heat. Add garlic and chicken; sauté 5 minutes. Combine coconut milk and next 4 ingredients, stirring with a whisk. Add coconut mixture to pan; bring to a simmer. Add broccoli and cauliflower; cover and cook 7 minutes or until vegetables are crisp-tender, stirring occasionally. Add chutney and pasta; toss well. Sprinkle with green onions, if desired. Yield: 6 servings (serving size: about 1⅓ cups).

CALORIES 216 (18% from fat); FAT 4.3g (sat 1.8g, mono 0.9g, poly 0.4g); PROTEIN 20g; CARB 25.9g; FIBER 3.6g; CHOL 44mg; IRON 1.9mg; SODIUM 724mg; CALC 52mg

The sweetness of the mango and the coconut milk tempers the heat of the curry, resulting in a complex, delicious dish. Though the chutney takes some time to make from scratch, the end result is worth the effort.

salads

Orzo Salad with Chickpeas, Dill, and Lemon

Versatile orzo, which means "barley" in Italian, is a common addition to sides, soups, and salads. The rice-shaped pasta is available in shorter, plumper "grains" and longer, thinner "grains."

1 cup uncooked orzo (rice-shaped pasta)
½ cup thinly sliced green onions
½ cup (2 ounces) crumbled feta cheese
¼ cup chopped fresh dill
1 (19-ounce) can chickpeas (garbanzo beans), rinsed and drained
3 tablespoons fresh lemon juice
1½ tablespoons extravirgin olive oil
1 tablespoon cold water
½ teaspoon salt
½ teaspoon bottled minced garlic

1. Cook pasta according to package directions, omitting salt and fat. Drain and rinse with cold water; drain.
2. Combine pasta, onions, cheese, dill, and chickpeas in a large bowl, tossing gently to combine.
3. Combine juice and remaining ingredients in a small bowl, stirring with a whisk. Drizzle over pasta mixture; toss gently to coat. Yield: 4 servings (serving size: 1¼ cups).

CALORIES 327 (29% from fat); FAT 10.4g (sat 2.9g, mono 5.1g, poly 1.8g); PROTEIN 10.8g; CARB 47.6g; FIBER 4.9g; CHOL 13mg; IRON 3mg; SODIUM 641mg; CALC 107mg

If you're not a big dill fan, use half the amount. Quick-cooking couscous can replace the orzo. When preparing the dressing, be sure your lemons are at room temperature; then, before juicing, roll them across the countertop while applying pressure with the palm of your hand. This method ensures that you get the most juice from each lemon.

Orecchiette with Tomatoes, Fresh Mozzarella, and Basil

2 cups uncooked orecchiette ("little ears" pasta)
3 cups chopped plum tomato
1¼ cups (5 ounces) diced fresh mozzarella cheese
1 cup loosely packed chopped fresh basil
1 tablespoon extravirgin olive oil
¾ teaspoon salt
¼ teaspoon crushed red pepper
2 garlic cloves, minced

1. Cook pasta according to package directions, omitting salt and fat; drain and rinse with cold water. Drain. Combine pasta, tomato, and remaining ingredients. Cover and chill at least 1 hour. Yield: 4 servings (serving size: 1½ cups).

CALORIES 376 (30% from fat); FAT 12.4g (sat 5.7g, mono 4.2g, poly 1.1g); PROTEIN 15.1g; CARB 50.5g; FIBER 3.4g; CHOL 28mg; IRON 3.4mg; SODIUM 361mg; CALC 239mg

Basil is one of the most important culinary herbs. Sweet basil, the most common type, is redolent of licorice and cloves. When married with tomatoes, as in this recipe, basil is at its best.

Taking its cue from Italy's insalata caprese, this easy make-ahead dish combines fresh mozzarella cheese with basil and tomatoes. Choose the ripest, most flavorful tomatoes for this sensational pasta salad.

Soba Noodle Salad with Vegetables and Tofu

To drain tofu (soybean curd), place it between several layers of paper towels, and press gently to wick away moisture. Make sure to buy firm tofu for this recipe so that it's solid enough to cut into cubes.

Dressing:

½ cup low-sodium soy sauce
¼ cup packed brown sugar
1 tablespoon sesame seeds, toasted
2 tablespoons orange juice
1 tablespoon bottled minced or minced peeled fresh ginger
1 tablespoon rice vinegar
2 teaspoons dark sesame oil
1 teaspoon bottled minced garlic
1 teaspoon chile paste with garlic

Salad:

4 cups hot cooked soba (about 8 ounces uncooked buckwheat noodles) or whole wheat spaghetti
3 cups very thinly sliced napa (Chinese) cabbage
2 cups fresh bean sprouts
1 cup shredded carrot
½ cup chopped fresh cilantro
1 (12.3-ounce) package firm tofu, drained and cut into 1-inch cubes

1. To prepare dressing, combine first 9 ingredients in a small bowl; stir with a whisk.

2. To prepare salad, combine noodles and remaining ingredients in a large bowl. Drizzle with dressing, tossing well to coat. Yield: 5 servings (serving size: 2 cups).

CALORIES 336 (19% from fat); FAT 7g (sat 1g, mono 1.8g, poly 3g); PROTEIN 15.1g; CARB 53.8g; FIBER 2.8g; CHOL 0mg; IRON 6.6mg; SODIUM 850mg; CALC 169mg

This Asian-inspired pasta salad keeps well in the refrigerator, so it's excellent to make ahead. If you're short on time, substitute bagged sliced cabbage or coleslaw mix for the napa cabbage.

Summer Farfalle
Salad with Smoked Salmon

Look for smoked salmon in vacuum-sealed packages near the gourmet cheeses or in the seafood department. Be sure to check the use-by date on the package, and buy the one that's farthest from expiration. There are many types of smoked salmon, but in general it should have a mild smoky flavor with firm flesh. Freeze leftover salmon for later use—sprinkle on scrambled eggs or add to a toasted bagel with light cream cheese.

  8 ounces uncooked farfalle (bow tie pasta)
  2 cups cherry tomatoes, halved
 ¼ cup chopped fresh dill
  1 (6-ounce) bag baby spinach
  1 teaspoon grated lemon rind
  2 tablespoons fresh lemon juice
  2 tablespoons cold water
 1½ tablespoons extravirgin olive oil
 ½ teaspoon salt
 ¼ teaspoon black pepper
  4 ounces (about 8 slices) smoked salmon, cut into thin strips

1. Cook pasta according to package directions, omitting salt and fat. Drain and rinse with cold water; drain.
2. Combine pasta, tomatoes, dill, and spinach in a large bowl, tossing gently.
3. Combine lemon rind and next 5 ingredients in a small bowl, stirring with a whisk. Drizzle over pasta mixture; toss gently to coat. Top with salmon. Yield: 6 servings (serving size: 2 cups).

CALORIES 206 (23% from fat); FAT 5.3g (sat 0.9g, mono 3.1g, poly 1.1g); PROTEIN 9.8g; CARB 31.4g; FIBER 2.7g; CHOL 4mg; IRON 2.3mg; SODIUM 603mg; CALC 43mg

Incorporating the best tastes of summer, this fresh salad is an ideal light supper on a hot day. Substitute leftover cooked salmon for the sliced smoked salmon, if you prefer.

Pasta Salad with Shrimp, Peppers, and Olives

Kalamata olives are large, purple-black Greek olives that are often slit before packing to allow better absorption of the olive oil and vinegar in which they're packed. They're juicy and plump with a powerful, bright acidity and high salt content. Just a small amount goes a long way in this dish.

2½ cups cooked angel hair (about 5 ounces uncooked pasta)
¾ cup chopped plum tomato
½ cup chopped red bell pepper
½ cup chopped yellow bell pepper
⅓ cup chopped green onions
2 tablespoons fresh lemon juice
1 tablespoon chopped pitted kalamata olives
1 tablespoon olive oil
1½ teaspoons chopped fresh or ½ teaspoon dried thyme
½ teaspoon white pepper
¼ teaspoon dried oregano
¾ pound cooked medium shrimp, peeled and deveined
1 garlic clove, minced
½ cup (2 ounces) crumbled feta cheese
1 tablespoon chopped fresh parsley

1. Combine first 13 ingredients in a large bowl. Sprinkle with cheese and parsley. Yield: 5 servings (serving size: 2 cups).

CALORIES 252 (26% from fat); FAT 7.2g (sat 2.4g, mono 2.9g, poly 1.1g); PROTEIN 19.8g; CARB 26.7g; FIBER 1.8g; CHOL 114mg; IRON 3.6mg; SODIUM 249mg; CALC 111mg

This Greek-style salad is perfect for casual entertaining. Serve it with a crisp wine and a side of bruschetta.

Seashells with Tuscan Tuna

Also known as sweet Italian onions, red onions lend a wonderful color and flavor to salads and pasta dishes. They're best eaten raw. When cooked, they lose their beautiful coloring and turn grayish brown. Pairing red onions with basil, as we have here, creates an especially vibrant taste.

8 ounces uncooked medium seashell pasta
½ cup chopped red onion
¼ cup thinly sliced fresh basil
2 tablespoons capers
2 tablespoons extravirgin olive oil
2 teaspoons grated lemon rind
½ teaspoon salt
¼ teaspoon freshly ground black pepper
2 (7.06-ounce) bags white albacore tuna in water

1. Cook pasta according to package directions, omitting salt and fat. Drain pasta in a colander over a bowl, reserving 2 tablespoons cooking liquid. Return pasta to pan. Add reserved cooking liquid, onion, and remaining ingredients; toss well. Yield: 4 servings (serving size: 1½ cups).

CALORIES 402 (24% from fat); FAT 10.6g (sat 1.9g, mono 5.8g, poly 1.7g); PROTEIN 31.8g; CARB 44.4g; FIBER 2.4g; CHOL 42mg; IRON 3.1mg; SODIUM 829mg; CALC 37mg

Tuna and red onion crostini are a favored snack on the menus of Florentine wine bars. The combination is tossed here with pasta shells. Look for tuna that's vacuum-sealed in bags—it's firmer than canned tuna and doesn't require draining.

Pappardelle with Tomatoes, Arugula, and Parmesan

Parmesan cheese is a hard, granular cheese that is so highly flavored that a little goes a long way, making it an excellent cheese for healthy cooking. Preshredded fresh Parmesan is fine for convenience, but for best flavor, grate or shave the cheese yourself. A cheese plane or a swivel-blade peeler works well for creating large shavings of cheese.

9 ounces uncooked pappardelle (wide ribbon pasta)
2 tablespoons extravirgin olive oil
¼ teaspoon crushed red pepper
3 garlic cloves, thinly sliced
1½ cups halved yellow tear-drop cherry tomatoes (pear-shaped)
1½ cups halved grape tomatoes
3 tablespoons fresh lemon juice
1 teaspoon salt
5 cups loosely packed trimmed arugula
⅓ cup (1½ ounces) shaved fresh Parmesan cheese
2 bacon slices, cooked and crumbled

1. Cook pasta according to package directions, omitting salt and fat. Drain; keep warm.

2. Heat oil in a large nonstick skillet over medium heat. Add pepper and garlic to pan; cook 1 minute or until garlic is fragrant. Add tomatoes; cook 45 seconds or just until heated, stirring gently. Remove pan from heat; stir in lemon juice and salt. Combine pasta, arugula, and tomato mixture in a large bowl, tossing to coat. Top with cheese and bacon. Yield: 4 servings (serving size: 2 cups).

CALORIES 388 (29% from fat); FAT 12.5g (sat 3.5g, mono 6.6g, poly 1.1g); PROTEIN 15.2g; CARB 55.7g; FIBER 3.8g; CHOL 10mg; IRON 3.1mg; SODIUM 828mg; CALC 189mg

If the cooked pasta clumps together, just rinse it under hot water, drain thoroughly, and then toss with the tomato mixture and arugula.

(pictured on cover)

Rotini, Summer Squash, and Prosciutto Salad with Rosemary Dressing

Dijon mustard is common as a sandwich spread, but it can work wonders in sauces and vinaigrettes, as in this rosemary dressing. It not only adds flavor, but also helps to bind the ingredients.

3 cups uncooked rotini (about 8 ounces corkscrew pasta)
1½ cups coarsely chopped yellow squash
1½ cups coarsely chopped zucchini
4 ounces thinly sliced prosciutto, chopped
3 tablespoons chopped red onion
2 ounces fresh mozzarella cheese, chopped
¼ teaspoon salt
¼ teaspoon freshly ground black pepper
2 tablespoons white balsamic vinegar
1 tablespoon extravirgin olive oil
1½ teaspoons Dijon mustard
½ teaspoon finely chopped fresh rosemary

1. Cook pasta according to package directions, omitting salt and fat. Add squash and zucchini during last minute of cooking. Drain pasta mixture; rinse with cold water.
2. Heat a large nonstick skillet over medium-high heat. Add prosciutto, and cook 5 minutes or until crisp, stirring frequently.
3. Combine pasta mixture, prosciutto, onion, and cheese in a large bowl; sprinkle with salt and pepper. Combine vinegar, oil, mustard, and rosemary in a small bowl, stirring with a whisk. Add vinegar mixture to pasta mixture, tossing gently to coat. Yield: 4 servings (serving size: 2¼ cups).

CALORIES 359 (28% from fat); FAT 11.1g (sat 4g, mono 2.8g, poly 0.4g); PROTEIN 18.7g; CARB 46.3g; FIBER 2.4g; CHOL 36mg; IRON 2.5mg; SODIUM 771mg; CALC 103mg

Using white balsamic vinegar maintains the salad dressing's pure golden color. Add the yellow squash and zucchini to the pasta during the last minute of cooking.

Chicken-Penne Salad with Green Beans

Vinegar can add depth of flavor and brightness to recipes, from salads to desserts. Red and white wine vinegars are stalwarts in the kitchen; they're versatile and work well in just about any dish. Wine vinegars, like wine itself, vary in flavor according to the type of grape from which they're made, where the grapes are grown, and how the vinegar is stored and aged.

2 cups uncooked penne (tube-shaped pasta)
2 cups (1-inch) cut green beans (about ½ pound)
2 cups shredded cooked chicken breast
½ cup vertically sliced red onion
¼ cup chopped fresh basil
1½ teaspoons chopped fresh flat-leaf parsley
1 (7-ounce) bottle roasted red bell pepper, drained and cut into thin strips
2 tablespoons extravirgin olive oil
2 tablespoons red wine vinegar
1 tablespoon cold water
½ teaspoon salt
½ teaspoon bottled minced garlic
¼ teaspoon black pepper

1. Cook pasta in boiling water 7 minutes. Add green beans; cook 4 minutes. Drain and rinse with cold water; drain.

2. Combine pasta mixture, chicken, and next 4 ingredients in a large bowl, tossing gently to combine.

3. Combine oil and remaining ingredients in a small bowl, stirring with a whisk. Drizzle over pasta mixture, and toss gently to coat. Yield: 4 servings (serving size: 2 cups).

CALORIES 384 (23% from fat); FAT 9.7g (sat 1.8g, mono 5.7g, poly 1.5g); PROTEIN 26.9g; CARB 47.8g; FIBER 2.6g; CHOL 49mg; IRON 3.2mg; SODIUM 866mg; CALC 59mg

Bottled roasted peppers and minced garlic save time without sacrificing flavor in this main-dish salad. Use two forks to shred the chicken breast. The texture of shredded chicken allows it to hold the dressing more easily.

world
cuisine

Fruited Israeli Couscous

2 teaspoons butter
1 cup finely chopped onion
½ cup dried currants
½ cup diced dried apricots
½ teaspoon salt
3 (14-ounce) cans fat-free, less-sodium chicken broth
3 (3-inch) cinnamon sticks
2½ cups uncooked Israeli couscous
¼ cup chopped fresh cilantro

1. Melt butter in a large saucepan over medium-high heat. Add onion, and sauté 5 minutes. Stir in currants and next 4 ingredients; bring to a boil. Add couscous, and return to a boil. Cover, reduce heat, and simmer 15 minutes. Let couscous mixture stand 5 minutes. Discard cinnamon sticks. Stir in cilantro. Yield: 12 servings (serving size: about ⅔ cup).

CALORIES 190 (4% from fat); FAT 0.9g (sat 0.4g, mono 0.2g, poly 0.1g); PROTEIN 6.5g; CARB 38.2g; FIBER 2.8g; CHOL 2mg; IRON 1mg; SODIUM 297mg; CALC 21mg

Although often considered a grain, couscous is really quick-cooking pasta made from semolina flour. Pearl-like Israeli couscous, also known as *maftoul*, has larger-sized grains than regular couscous and takes on the consistency of macaroni when prepared. It cooks longer than regular couscous due to its size, but its size also allows it to absorb plenty of liquid and flavor. Look for this Israeli import in specialty and Middle Eastern markets.

The only tools this recipe requires are a saucepan, a cutting board, and a knife. Cinnamon sticks steeped in the cooking liquid lend warm spiciness to the couscous and dried fruit.

Peanutty Noodles

Natural peanut butter is the kind with a layer of oil on top, which needs to be stirred back into the peanut butter before using. Although it's not as creamy as regular peanut butter, it doesn't have trans fatty acids and is high in healthy monounsaturated fat. Natural peanut butter has more peanut flavor and works perfectly in this sauce.

2 carrots, peeled
1 tablespoon vegetable oil, divided
2 teaspoons grated peeled fresh ginger
3 garlic cloves, minced
1 cup fat-free, less-sodium chicken broth
½ cup natural-style peanut butter (such as Smucker's)
¼ cup low-sodium soy sauce
3 tablespoons rice or white wine vinegar
1 teaspoon chili garlic sauce (such as Lee Kum Kee)
¼ teaspoon salt
Cooking spray
2 cups red bell pepper strips
1 pound snow peas, trimmed
8 cups hot cooked linguine (about 1 pound uncooked pasta)
½ cup chopped fresh cilantro (optional)

1. Shave carrots lengthwise into thin strips using a vegetable peeler, and set aside.
2. Heat 1 teaspoon oil in a small saucepan over medium heat. Add ginger and minced garlic; sauté 30 seconds. Add chicken broth and next 5 ingredients; stir until well blended. Reduce heat, and simmer 7 minutes, stirring occasionally. Remove from heat, and keep warm.
3. Heat 2 teaspoons oil in a large nonstick skillet coated with cooking spray over medium-high heat. Add bell peppers and snow peas; sauté 5 minutes or until tender. Remove from heat. Combine carrot, peanut butter mixture, bell pepper mixture, and linguine in a large bowl; toss well. Sprinkle with cilantro, if desired. Serve immediately. Yield: 10 servings (serving size: 1 cup).

CALORIES 296 (27% from fat); FAT 8.8g (sat 1.7g, mono 3.8g, poly 2.7g); PROTEIN 11.7g; CARB 43.1g; FIBER 3.4g; CHOL 1mg; IRON 3.6mg; SODIUM 400mg; CALC 44mg

Though peanut sauce has become popular in Thai-American cuisine, it's actually Malaysian or Indonesian in origin. It's used as a dip for satay skewers, in salads, and to dress noodles, as in this recipe. This dish can be served as a main dish or as a side dish with pork, chicken, or shrimp.

Singapore Mai Fun

To peel fresh ginger, you can use a vegetable peeler or a paring knife, but a teaspoon also works well: Hold the ginger on a work surface, and move the tip of the spoon lengthwise across the ginger to scrape off the skin.

1 (6-ounce) package skinny rice noodles (*py mai fun*)
½ cup fat-free, less-sodium chicken broth
3 tablespoons low-sodium soy sauce
1 teaspoon sugar
½ teaspoon salt
Cooking spray
1 tablespoon peanut oil, divided
1 large egg, lightly beaten
½ cup red bell pepper strips
1 tablespoon grated peeled fresh ginger
¼ teaspoon crushed red pepper
3 garlic cloves, minced
8 ounces skinless, boneless chicken breast, thinly sliced
1 tablespoon curry powder
8 ounces medium shrimp, peeled and deveined
1 cup (1-inch) slices green onions

1. Cook rice noodles according to package directions, omitting salt and fat. Drain.

2. Combine broth, soy sauce, sugar, and salt; stir until sugar dissolves.

3. Heat a large nonstick skillet over medium-high heat; coat pan with cooking spray. Add 1 teaspoon oil. Add egg; stir-fry 30 seconds or until soft-scrambled, stirring constantly. Remove from pan. Wipe pan clean with a paper towel. Heat 2 teaspoons oil in pan over medium-high heat. Add bell pepper strips, ginger, crushed red pepper, and garlic; stir-fry 15 seconds. Add chicken, and stir-fry 2 minutes. Add curry and shrimp; stir-fry 2 minutes. Stir in noodles, broth mixture, and egg; cook 1 minute or until thoroughly heated. Sprinkle with green onions. Yield: 6 servings (serving size: 1 cup).

CALORIES 237 (17% from fat); FAT 4.6g (sat 1g, mono 1.7g, poly 1.3g); PROTEIN 19.7g; CARB 27.8g; FIBER 1.3g; CHOL 115mg; IRON 2.2mg; SODIUM 646mg; CALC 53mg

A favorite on Chinese take-out menus, this curried noodle dish is a sure hit and ready in a snap—provided you have the ingredients prepped before you start. The leftovers are good cold, as well. You'll find skinny rice noodles in the supermarket's ethnic food section.

Ginger Shrimp with Carrot Couscous

For best flavor, use freshly squeezed lime juice. Buy limes that are plump and heavy for their size. You'll get more juice out of a lime if you bring it to room temperature before juicing. Use your hands, a reamer, or a citrus press to extract the juice. One medium lime will give you about 1½ tablespoons of juice. You'll need 4 limes for this recipe.

1 tablespoon vegetable oil, divided
1 (12-ounce) can carrot juice, divided
¾ cup uncooked couscous
¼ cup fresh lime juice
2 to 3 teaspoons minced seeded jalapeño pepper
2 teaspoons grated peeled fresh ginger
¼ teaspoon salt
¼ cup sliced green onions
4 cups gourmet salad greens
1½ pounds cooked, peeled, and deveined medium shrimp

1. Combine 1 teaspoon oil and 1 cup carrot juice in a medium saucepan; bring to a boil. Gradually stir in couscous. Remove from heat. Cover and let stand 5 minutes.
2. While couscous stands, bring remaining carrot juice to a boil in a small saucepan; cook until reduced to ¼ cup (about 2½ minutes). Remove from heat; stir in 2 teaspoons oil, lime juice, jalapeño, ginger, and salt.
3. Fluff couscous with a fork; stir in ¼ cup reduced carrot juice mixture and onions. Combine remaining carrot juice mixture, greens, and shrimp in a bowl, tossing gently to coat. Place couscous mixture on each of 4 plates; top with shrimp mixture. Yield: 4 servings (serving size: about ½ cup couscous mixture and 1½ cups shrimp mixture).

CALORIES 403 (13% from fat); FAT 5.8g (sat 1.1g, mono 1.2g, poly 3g); PROTEIN 42.7g; CARB 43.4g; FIBER 4.2g; CHOL 332mg; IRON 6.9mg; SODIUM 572mg; CALC 133mg

Carrot juice is the secret ingredient in this supereasy recipe. The juice gives the couscous vibrant color and packs this dish with more than 100 percent of the daily recommended amount of vitamin A. Carrots, first cultivated in West Africa and the eastern Mediterranean, are a natural complement to couscous, a staple food in the same area of the world.

Hanoi Beef and Rice Noodle Soup

Star anise, a star-shaped, eight-pointed, dark brown pod, comes from a Chinese evergreen tree related to the magnolia. Each anise pod contains eight seeds that are more bitter than regular anise seeds. Star anise is used in Asian cooking to flavor teas; Westerners use it to flavor liqueurs and baked goods. It can be found whole in Asian markets and some supermarkets and is ground for an ingredient in Chinese five-spice powder.

Broth:

- 3 pounds beef oxtail
- ¾ cup thinly sliced peeled fresh ginger (about 3 ounces)
- ⅔ cup coarsely chopped shallots (about 3 medium shallots)
- 5 quarts water
- 4 cups coarsely chopped daikon radish (about 1 pound)
- 3 tablespoons Thai fish sauce (such as Three Crabs)
- 2 tablespoons sugar
- 1 teaspoon white peppercorns
- 5 whole cloves
- 2 star anise
- 1 large yellow onion, peeled and quartered
- 1 cinnamon stick

Remaining ingredients:

- 2 cups vertically sliced onion
- 12 ounces wide rice stick noodles (*bánh pho*)
- 2 cups fresh bean sprouts
- 12 ounces eye-of-round roast, trimmed and cut into ¹⁄₁₆-inch slices
- 2 cups cilantro leaves
- 1 cup Thai basil leaves
- 4 red Thai chiles, seeded and thinly sliced
- 8 lime wedges
- 1 tablespoon hoisin sauce (optional)

1. To prepare broth, heat a large stockpot over medium-high heat. Add oxtail, ginger, and shallots; sauté 8 minutes or until ginger and shallots are slightly charred. Add water and next 8 ingredients; bring to a boil. Reduce heat, and simmer 4 hours. Strain broth through a sieve into a large bowl; discard solids. Return broth to pan; bring to a boil. Reduce heat to medium, and cook until reduced to 10 cups (about 30 minutes). Skim fat from surface; discard fat. Keep warm.

2. To prepare remaining ingredients, add sliced onion to broth. Place noodles in a large bowl, and cover with boiling water. Let stand 20 minutes. Drain. Place ⅓ cup bean sprouts in each of 6 soup bowls. Top each serving with 1⅓ cups noodles and 2 ounces eye-of-round. Bring broth to a boil; carefully ladle 1⅔ cups boiling broth over each serving (boiling broth will cook meat). Serve with cilantro, basil, chiles, limes, and hoisin, if desired. Yield: 6 servings.

CALORIES 404 (19% from fat); FAT 8.5g (sat 3.3g, mono 3.7g, poly 0.5g); PROTEIN 23.4g; CARB 58g; FIBER 3.5g; CHOL 57mg; IRON 3.3mg; SODIUM 751mg; CALC 69mg

Traditionally a northern Vietnamese breakfast specialty, pho bo—a beef and noodle soup—is now eaten at any time of day. Partially freeze the eye-of-round roast to make it easier to slice. You can also use regular sweet basil in place of Thai basil.

Cinnamon-Beef Noodles

Cinnamon and ginger may be more familiar in sweet dishes, but many cultures use them in savory dishes as well. Cinnamon sticks add a subtle sweet heat while the warm, slightly woody flavor of ginger adds an herbal liveliness. Garlic is very pungent and the more it's chopped, the stronger it tastes. Together these seasonings provide an extra kick of flavor when added to the rice wine and soy sauce mixture.

5 cups water
1½ cups rice wine or sake
¾ cup low-sodium soy sauce
¼ cup sugar
2 teaspoons vegetable oil, divided
2 pounds beef stew meat, cut into 1½-inch cubes
8 green onions, cut into 1-inch pieces
6 garlic cloves, crushed
2 cinnamon sticks
1 (1-inch) piece peeled fresh ginger, thinly sliced
1 (10-ounce) package fresh spinach, chopped
4 cups hot cooked wide lo mein noodles or vermicelli (about 8 ounces uncooked pasta)

1. Combine first 4 ingredients in a large bowl; stir with a whisk. Set aside.

2. Heat 1 teaspoon oil in a large Dutch oven over medium-high heat; add half of beef, browning on all sides. Remove from pan. Repeat procedure with 1 teaspoon oil and remaining beef. Return beef to pan; add water mixture, onions, garlic, cinnamon, and ginger. Bring to a boil; cover, reduce heat, and simmer 2 hours or until beef is tender. Discard ginger slices and cinnamon. Stir in spinach; cook 3 minutes or until wilted. Serve over noodles. Yield: 8 servings (serving size: 1 cup beef mixture and ½ cup noodles).

CALORIES 403 (14% from fat); FAT 6.2g (sat 2.3g, mono 3.3g, poly 1.3g); PROTEIN 30.5g; CARB 50.4g; FIBER 2.9g; CHOL 44mg; IRON 5.2mg; SODIUM 1,080mg; CALC 80mg

This Chinese dish can be compared to a Western stew. It's a classic example of red-cooking, a method in which meat is simmered in a soy sauce–based mixture for a long time until tender. It can be used to cook a variety of meats, including pork, lamb, chicken, and duck.

North African Chicken and Couscous

Fresh and dried fruits such as apricots, dates, figs, raisins, and nuts are basic foods in many countries bordering the Mediterranean. They're often used to enhance the flavors of savory dishes. Moist, golden raisins add a hint of sweetness to this couscous.

2 cups water
1½ cups uncooked couscous
½ cup golden raisins
½ cup thawed orange juice concentrate, undiluted
⅓ cup lemon juice
2 tablespoons water
2 tablespoons olive oil
2 teaspoons ground cumin
½ teaspoon salt
¼ teaspoon black pepper
3 cups chopped ready-to-eat roasted skinless, boneless chicken breast (about 3 breasts)
2 cups chopped peeled cucumber
1 cup chopped red bell pepper
¼ cup thinly sliced green onions
½ cup chopped fresh cilantro
Sliced green onions (optional)

1. Bring water to a boil in a medium saucepan, and gradually stir in couscous and raisins. Remove from heat. Cover; let stand 5 minutes. Fluff with a fork.
2. Combine orange juice and next 6 ingredients; stir well with a whisk.
3. Combine couscous mixture, juice mixture, chicken, and next 4 ingredients in a large bowl, and toss well. Garnish with green onions, if desired. Yield: 6 servings (serving size: 2 cups).

CALORIES 332 (18% from fat); FAT 6.6g (sat 1.2g, mono 3g, poly 0.9g); PROTEIN 19.6g; CARB 51.2g; FIBER 3.3g; CHOL 35mg; IRON 2.8mg; SODIUM 498mg; CALC 51mg

Couscous, cumin, and cilantro are common elements in North African cuisine, as is the combination of savory and sweet. This dish makes a quick weeknight meal.

Spicy Asian Lettuce Wraps

2½ ounces bean threads
(cellophane noodles)
¼ cup minced fresh cilantro
¼ cup low-sodium soy sauce
1 tablespoon chile paste with
garlic
2 teaspoons dark sesame oil
2 cups chopped roasted
skinless, boneless chicken
breast
12 large Boston or romaine
lettuce leaves

1. Cover bean threads with boiling water. Let stand 5 minutes or until softened. Drain and rinse with cool water. Chop noodles.
2. While bean threads soak, combine cilantro, soy sauce, chile paste, and oil in a large bowl, stirring with a whisk. Add noodles and chicken to soy sauce mixture; toss well to coat. Spoon about ⅓ cup chicken mixture down center of each lettuce leaf; roll up. Yield: 4 servings (serving size: 3 lettuce wraps).

CALORIES 213 (21% from fat); FAT 4.9g (sat 1g, mono 1.8g, poly 1.5g); PROTEIN 23.2g; CARB 18.3g; FIBER 0.7g; CHOL 60mg; IRON 1.7mg; SODIUM 641mg; CALC 31mg

Translucent cellophane noodles are known by a variety of names, including bean threads, Chinese vermicelli, glass noodles, and *bai fun*. Unlike most "pastas," cellophane noodles are made from the starch of mung beans rather than wheat. Instead of boiling, soak them briefly in hot water to soften before serving.

Lettuce wraps have become quite the rage at many restaurants, but can be high in sodium. This homemade version uses low-sodium soy sauce and just 2 teaspoons of flavor-packed sesame oil for a healthier dish. You can increase or decrease the chile paste to suit your taste.

Peanut Chicken Soba Salad

Soba noodles are protein-rich noodles native to Japan and made from a combination of buckwheat flour (*soba-ko*) and wheat flour (*komugi-ko*). Look for soba noodles in the ethnic or pasta section of natural food and grocery stores, or in specialty Asian markets. Although fettuccine or linguine can be used in place of soba noodles, these are one of the few Asian noodles for which there really is no suitable substitute.

2 cups water
2 (6-ounce) skinless, boneless chicken breast halves
4 black peppercorns
1 bay leaf
2 tablespoons roasted peanut oil
1 tablespoon rice vinegar
2 teaspoons low-sodium soy sauce
1 teaspoon honey
1 teaspoon chili garlic sauce (such as Lee Kum Kee)
½ teaspoon salt
2 cups cooked soba noodles (about 4 ounces uncooked)
1 cup grated carrot
½ cup thinly sliced green onions
¼ cup minced red onion
¼ cup chopped fresh basil
4 teaspoons chopped unsalted, dry-roasted peanuts
Lime wedges (optional)

1. Combine first 4 ingredients in a medium saucepan; bring to a boil. Cover, remove from heat, and let stand 15 minutes or until chicken is done. Remove chicken from pan, and discard peppercorns, bay leaf, and cooking liquid. Shred chicken; place in a large bowl.
2. Combine oil and next 5 ingredients, stirring with a whisk. Pour over chicken; let stand 5 minutes. Add soba noodles and next 4 ingredients to chicken mixture, and toss well. Sprinkle with peanuts. Garnish with lime wedges, if desired. Yield: 4 servings (serving size: 1 cup salad and 1 teaspoon peanuts).

CALORIES 256 (33% from fat); FAT 9.5g (sat 1.7g, mono 4.2g, poly 2.9g); PROTEIN 23.9g; CARB 19.5g; FIBER 2.5g; CHOL 49mg; IRON 1.3mg; SODIUM 538mg; CALC 30mg

You'll only need about 15 minutes to cook the chicken and noodles for this Asian salad. If short on time, substitute rotisserie chicken or leftover cooked chicken, and purchase preshredded carrots from your supermarket's produce section.

all about
Pasta

In this Cooking Class, you'll find answers to the most frequently asked questions about pasta and must-have information on selecting, preparing, and serving it—as well as recipes for essential sauces. There's no magic required, just loving attention.

Purchasing Pasta

Once pasta is incorporated into a recipe, the different brands all taste about the same, so don't pay more for a fancy name, domestic or imported. What does matter is choosing the right noodle for your dish and cooking it properly.

Dried and Fresh Pasta

• *Dried pasta* is a mixture of water and semolina. In factories, the mix is made into a paste that's turned into different shapes by passing through dies, or large metal discs filled with holes. The pasta is then dried and packaged. When cooked, dried pasta has a nutty wheat flavor and pleasant chewy bite. The *Cooking Light* Test Kitchens mostly use dried pasta in recipes.

• *Fresh pasta* is made with regular soft wheat flour, or a combination of other flours, and eggs, giving it a rich flavor and silky texture. It's perishable, so it's

generally pricier than dried. Fresh pasta cooks quickly, 2 to 3 minutes on average, making it a handy substitution when you're short on time.

Pasta Shapes

Many varieties of pasta are interchangeable if similar in shape and size (see categories below). There are also specially shaped pastas, like lasagna (also available in "no-boil" form) and manicotti, that are used in baked dishes. Ravioli and tortellini are filled with meat, cheese, or other ingredients.

Long thin shapes
• angel hair
• fettuccine (small ribbons)
• linguine
• spaghetti
• spaghettini
• vermicelli

Long wide shape
• pappardelle

Twisted and curved shapes
• cavatappi
• elbow macaroni (gomiti)
• farfalle (bow ties)
• fusilli (short twisted spaghetti)
• orecchiette ("little ears")
• radiatore

• rotelle (wheels)
• rotini (corkscrews)
• seashell macaroni

Tubular shapes
• ditalini
• mezzani
• mostaccioli
• penne
• rigatoni
• ziti

Pastinas (small pastas)
• couscous
• orzo (rice-shaped pasta)
• pennette
• tubetti

Note: Ridged pastas will have "rigati" or "rigate" added to their names.

Essential Tips for Cooking Pasta

Cooking pasta is fairly simple, and most packages give directions. Here are some additional recommendations from our staff.

• **Put the water on to boil** before beginning the rest of the recipe.

• **Fill a large pot, such as a Dutch oven or stock pot,** with enough water so the pasta can move freely while cooking. (Too little water may cause uneven cooking; too much might overflow.) For 8 ounces of dried pasta, you'll need to use a 4-quart pot.

• **Cover the pot, and bring the water to a full rolling boil** over high heat.

• It's not necessary to add oil or salt to the cooking water. Sauce won't adhere as well to the pasta's surface when it's cooked with oil. Salt does make pasta taste better on its own, but when it's tossed with a flavorful sauce, there's no need to add extra sodium.

• **Add the pasta, and stir with a pasta fork.** When the water returns to a rolling boil, start the timer. Stir often. If you use fresh pasta, remember that it cooks more quickly than dried.

• **Always cook pasta uncovered** over high heat.

• **Start testing for doneness** a few minutes before the indicated cooking time.

• **Perfectly cooked pasta has a firm, tender consistency, called "al dente,"** Italian for "to the tooth." When testing for doneness, remove a piece of pasta from the water and bite into it. It should offer resistance to the bite but have no trace of brittleness. If an undercooked piece of pasta is cut in half, a white dot or line is clearly visible in the center. Al dente pasta has only a speck of white remaining, meaning the pasta has absorbed just enough water to hydrate it. Cook pasta slightly less than al dente if you're going to cook it for additional time with the sauce.

undercooked pasta (left), al dente pasta (middle), overcooked pasta (right)

• **Set a large colander in the sink** so the water drains quickly.

• **Do not rinse cooked pasta** unless the recipe specifically calls for you to do so. Rinsing washes away some of the starch, making it less sticky. Less starch is ideal for pasta salads that benefit from less stickiness once chilled. But that starch helps the sauce adhere to warm or freshly cooked pasta.

• **Return the pasta to the warm cooking pot** or add to the skillet with the sauce; toss immediately with large tongs or a pasta fork.

• **Pasta can be tricky to serve** because it has a tendency to slip and slide. The best serving utensil, especially for longer pasta, is a metal or wooden pasta fork or tongs. For short pasta, a large slotted spoon works fine.

Amounts of Dry and Cooked Pasta

Use this guide to help you determine either how much pasta you'll need or how much you'll get. Approximate cooking times are also included.

Type	Dry Weight (8 ounces)	Cooked Volume	Cooking Time
Acini de pepe (small balls similar to orzo)	1¼ cups	3 cups	5 minutes
Alphabets	2 cups	4 cups	5 minutes
Capellini or angel hair	8 ounces	3½ cups	5 minutes
Cavatappi	3 cups	5 cups	8 minutes
Conchiglie rigate (seashell pasta)	3 cups	4 cups	14 minutes
Egg noodles, medium	4 cups	5 cups	5 minutes
Egg noodles, wide	4½ cups	5 cups	5 minutes
Elbow macaroni	2 cups	4 cups	5 minutes
Farfalle (bow tie pasta)	3 cups	4 cups	11 minutes
Fettuccine	8 ounces	4 cups	10 minutes
Fusilli (short twisted spaghetti)	3 cups	4 cups	10 minutes
Gemelli	2 cups	4 cups	10 minutes
Linguine	8 ounces	4 cups	10 minutes
Orecchiette ("little ears" pasta)	2½ cups	4 cups	11 minutes
Orzo (rice-shaped pasta)	1¼ cups	2½ cups	6 minutes
Penne or mostaccioli (tube-shaped pasta)	2 cups	4 cups	10 minutes
Penne rigate	2 cups	4 cups	10 minutes
Perciatelli	8 ounces	4 cups	11 minutes
Radiatore (short coiled pasta)	3 cups	4½ cups	10 minutes
Rigatoni	2½ cups	4 cups	10 minutes
Rotini (corkscrew pasta)	4 cups	4 cups	10 minutes
Small seashell pasta	2 cups	4 cups	8 minutes
Spaghetti	8 ounces	3½ cups	10 minutes
Vermicelli	8 ounces	4 cups	5 minutes
Ziti (short tube-shaped pasta)	3 cups	4 cups	10 minutes

Essential Techniques for Making Pasta

A simple mixture of flour and eggs, such as the recipe at right, creates a versatile paste that can be shaped, cut, and cooked in a variety of ways. Here, we show you how to make fettuccine. (To make dough in a food processor: Place flour and salt in processor; pulse 3 times or until combined. With processor on, slowly add eggs through food chute; process until dough forms a ball. Follow the essential techniques starting with 4.)

The Dough

1. Make a well in center of flour mixture, and add eggs.

2. Stir egg with a fork to gradually incorporate flour and form a dough.

3. Turn dough out onto a lightly floured surface; shape into a ball.

4. Knead until smooth and elastic (about 10 to 15 minutes).

5. Wrap dough in plastic wrap; let rest 10 minutes.

The Noodles

6. Pass dough through smooth rollers of pasta machine, beginning on widest setting.

7. Pass dough through cutting rollers of machine.

8. Hang pasta on a wooden drying rack.

Homemade Fettuccine

1¼ cups plus 1 tablespoon
    all-purpose flour, divided
½ teaspoon salt
2 large eggs, lightly beaten

1. Lightly spoon flour into dry measuring cups; level with a knife. Combine 1 cup flour and salt. Make a well in center of mixture. Add eggs; stir with a fork to gradually incorporate flour into a dough.
2. Turn dough out onto a lightly floured surface; shape into a ball. Knead until smooth and elastic; add enough of remaining flour, 1 tablespoon at a time, to prevent dough from sticking to hands. Wrap in plastic wrap; let rest 10 minutes.
3. Divide dough into 4 equal portions. Working with 1 portion at a time (cover remaining dough with plastic wrap to keep from drying), pass through smooth rollers of pasta machine on widest setting. Continue moving width gauge to narrower settings; pass dough through rollers at each setting, brushing lightly with flour if needed to prevent sticking.
4. Roll dough to about ¹⁄₁₆ inch. Pass through fettuccine cutting rollers of machine. Hang on a wooden drying rack (dry no longer than 30 minutes). Repeat procedure with remaining dough.
5. Bring 3 quarts water to a rolling boil. Add pasta; cook 2 to 4 minutes or until "al dente." Drain; serve immediately. Yield: 6 servings (serving size: ½ cup).

CALORIES 125 (14% from fat); FAT 1.9g (sat 0.6g, mono 0.7g, poly 0.3g); PROTEIN 4.9g; CARB 21.2g; FIBER 0.7g; CHOL 71mg; IRON 1.5mg; SODIUM 217mg; CALC 12mg

World of Pasta

Often when we think of pasta, we think of Italian pasta, made from a durum wheat flour, called semolina, and water. Pastas from other cultures, with different tastes, textures, and ingredients, open up a whole new world of possibilities.

Asia

Cellophane noodles: Also called bean threads, these translucent dried noodles are made from the starch of mung beans, potatoes, or green peas.

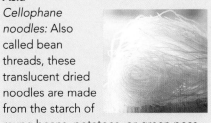

Chinese egg noodles: Chinese egg noodles are usually made from a dough of wheat flour, eggs, and salt. If they don't contain eggs, they may be labeled "imitation" or "egg-flavored."

Chinese wheat-flour noodles: These noodles are made with flour and water. Many stores offer a wide variety of "flavored" noodles (shrimp, crab, and chicken), and they may be round or flat.

Rice Sticks: The most popular of all Asian noodles, rice sticks are made from rice flour and water. Although any type of rice-flour noodle may be called rice sticks, we use this term for flat rice noodles, which are sold mainly in three forms. Thin flat rice noodles most often are used in soups and in some stir-fried dishes. Medium-thick rice sticks (called

pho in Vietnamese) are all-purpose and may be used in soups, stir-fries, and salads (a slightly wider Thai version is called *jantaboon*). The widest rice sticks (*sha he fen* in Chinese) are used in meat, seafood, and vegetable stir-fries.

Soba: Soba noodles from Japan are made with a combination of buckwheat flour, wheat flour, and water. This is one of the few Asian noodles for which there is no substitute.

Somen: The most delicate of noodles, somen are made with wheat flour, a dash of oil, and water. They're served cold with a dipping sauce or hot in soups. The closest substitution would be a very fine pasta, such as capellini or vermicelli.

North Africa

Couscous: Regarded by many as a grain, couscous is actually a pasta made from semolina (durum wheat) flour and salted water. In Tunisia, Algeria, and Morocco, where it's a national favorite, couscous ranges in size from fine- to medium-grained. Another variety, Israeli couscous, is larger.

The Essential Sauce

It's almost impossible to think of pasta without thinking of sauce. And though there are some wonderful convenience products on the market, sometimes nothing can compare to homemade.

We've included classic versions of Alfredo, marinara, carbonara, and clam sauce in the Essential Pasta chapter, but here are a few more sauces that no pasta lover should be without.

How to Sauce Pasta

When saucing pasta, think of the sauce as a seasoning or dressing that you toss with the pasta, much like a salad and dressing, until each piece of pasta is moist. The idea is to impart well-flavored seasoning to each bite of the finished dish.

Long shapes are generally most compatible with smoother sauces that coat them all over (think of the perfect marriage of fettuccine and Alfredo). Short shapes work well with chunky sauces that can be caught in the nooks and crannies.

Quick-and-Easy Tomato Sauce

Use this sauce anywhere you might use a store-bought sauce, such as on pasta, in lasagna, or over polenta. Chop the tomatoes in the can with kitchen shears.

  1 tablespoon olive oil
1½ cups chopped onion
  1 cup chopped green bell pepper
  1 teaspoon dried oregano
  4 garlic cloves, minced
  ½ cup dry red wine
  1 teaspoon dried basil
  ½ teaspoon salt
  ¼ teaspoon black pepper
  2 (28-ounce) cans whole plum tomatoes, undrained and chopped
  1 (6-ounce) can tomato paste
  2 bay leaves

1. Heat oil in a large saucepan over medium-high heat. Add onion, bell pepper, oregano, and garlic; cook 5 minutes or until vegetables are tender, stirring occasionally.
2. Add wine and remaining ingredients, and bring to a boil. Reduce heat, and simmer 30 minutes. Discard bay leaves. Yield: 8 cups (serving size: 1 cup).

CALORIES 93 (23% from fat); FAT 2.4g (sat 0.4g, mono 1.4g, poly 0.5g); PROTEIN 3.3g; CARB 17.1g; FIBER 3.3g; CHOL 0mg; IRON 2.4mg; SODIUM 487mg; CALC 77mg

Mushroom Sauce

The combination of dried porcini and cremini mushrooms and red wine creates a hearty, "meaty" flavor in this meat-free sauce. Toss it with cavatappi or any other short spiral pasta.

1½ cups dried porcini mushrooms (about 1½ ounces)
  2 teaspoons olive oil
  ½ cup finely chopped prosciutto (about 2 ounces)
  ½ cup finely chopped onion
  4 cups sliced cremini or button mushrooms (about 8 ounces)
  ½ teaspoon grated lemon rind
  ½ teaspoon salt
  ¼ teaspoon pepper
  2 garlic cloves, minced
  1 cup fat-free, less-sodium chicken broth
  ¾ cup dry red wine
  1 tablespoon cornstarch
  1 tablespoon water

1. Place porcini mushrooms in a bowl; add boiling water to cover. Cover and let stand 30 minutes. Drain; rinse and coarsely chop mushrooms.
2. Heat oil in a medium skillet over medium-high heat. Add prosciutto; sauté 1 minute. Add onion; sauté 3 minutes or until tender. Stir in porcini and cremini mushrooms and next 4 ingredients; cook 4 minutes or until browned, stirring frequently. Stir in broth and wine, scraping pan to loosen browned bits. Bring to a boil, and cook 3 minutes. Combine

cornstarch and 1 tablespoon water. Add cornstarch mixture to pan; bring to a boil. Cook 1 minute, stirring constantly. Yield: 4 servings (serving size: 1 cup).

CALORIES 125 (32% from fat); FAT 4.5g (sat 1g, mono 1.9g, poly 0.4g); PROTEIN 9.2g; CARB 12.5g; FIBER 2.2g; CHOL 13mg; IRON 2.9mg; SODIUM 735mg; CALC 17mg

Pesto

Pesto means "pounded," which refers to the tra-ditional preparation using a mortar and pestle. It's an uncooked sauce of fresh basil, garlic, olive oil, pine nuts, and Parmesan and Romano cheeses. Our pesto has half the fat and calories of the typical recipe. When tossing pesto with pasta, add about 3 tablespoons of the pasta cooking liquid. (pictured on opposite page)

    2 ounces fresh Parmesan cheese,
       cut into pieces
 ½ ounce fresh Romano cheese, cut
       into pieces
    2 garlic cloves, peeled
    4 cups fresh basil leaves
    2 tablespoons pine nuts
    2 tablespoons extravirgin olive oil
    2 teaspoons butter, softened
 ¼ teaspoon salt

1. Place cheeses in a food processor; process until finely grated. Add garlic; process until minced. Add basil and remaining ingredients; process until blended. Yield: 4 servings (serving size: ¼ cup).

CALORIES 192 (78% from fat); FAT 16.7g (sat 5.1g, mono 8g, poly 2.6g); PROTEIN 8.2g; CARB 3.6g; FIBER 1.8g; CHOL 21mg; IRON 2mg; SODIUM 417mg; CALC 260mg

Spaghetti Aglio e Olio

In Italian, aglio e olio (AH-lyoh ay OH-lyoh) means "garlic and oil." Typically, the garlic is fried in olive oil on the stovetop, but we've cooked it in the microwave; it's easier and omits the risk of burning the garlic. Add some crushed red pepper flakes for a spicier version. (pictured on page 7)

    2 tablespoons extravirgin olive oil
 ¼ teaspoon dried oregano
    4 large garlic cloves, minced
    4 quarts water
    8 ounces uncooked spaghetti
 ½ cup fat-free, less-sodium chicken
       broth
    2 tablespoons minced fresh parsley

1. Combine olive oil, oregano, and minced garlic in a small microwave-safe bowl. Cover bowl with wax paper, and microwave at HIGH 1 minute.
2. Bring water to a boil in a large stock-pot. Add spaghetti; return to a boil. Cook, uncovered, 10 minutes or until al dente, stirring occasionally. Drain. Return to pot. Stir in garlic mixture and broth. Cook over medium heat 4 min-utes or until broth is absorbed, stirring constantly. Stir in parsley. Yield: 4 serv-ings (serving size: 1 cup).

CALORIES 278 (25% from fat); FAT 7.7g (sat 1.0g, mono 5.1g, poly 1.0g); PROTEIN 7.9g; CARB 43.7g; FIBER 1.5g; CHOL 0mg; IRON 2.4mg; SODIUM 66mg; CALC 20mg

Smoky Marinara

Look for fire-roasted tomatoes (we used Muir Glen) in the organic section or with the canned tomatoes in your supermarket. This recipe accom-panies Four-Cheese Stuffed Shells on page 80, or toss it with penne or other tubular shapes.

    1 tablespoon olive oil
    3 garlic cloves, minced
 ¼ cup chopped fresh basil
    2 tablespoons chopped fresh parsley
    2 tablespoons chopped fresh or
       2 teaspoons dried oregano
    2 teaspoons balsamic vinegar
 ⅛ teaspoon salt
 ⅛ teaspoon pepper
    1 (28-ounce) can crushed fire-
       roasted tomatoes, undrained
    1 (28-ounce) can crushed tomatoes,
       undrained

1. Heat oil in a large saucepan over medium heat. Add garlic, basil, parsley, and oregano; sauté 1 minute, stirring frequently. Stir in vinegar and remain-ing ingredients. Reduce heat, and sim-mer 10 minutes. Yield: 6 cups (serving size: ½ cup).

CALORIES 55 (20% from fat); FAT 1.2g (sat 0.2g, mono 0.8g, poly 0.1g); PROTEIN 2.3g; CARB 9g; FIBER 2.3g; CHOL 0mg; IRON 0.9mg; SODIUM 350mg; CALC 49mg

Subject Index

Recipe Index